the
Clueless
Baker

D0472576

Also by Evelyn Raab

Clueless in the Kitchen
The Clueless Vegetarian

the Clueless Baker

Baking from Scratch—Easy as Pie

EVELYN RAAB

FIREFLY BOOKS

A FIREFLY BOOK

Published by Firefly Books (U.S.) Inc. 2001

Copyright © 2001 by Evelyn Raab

All rights reserved. No part of this publication may be reproduced, stored in a retrieval system or transmitted in any form or by any means, electronic, mechanical, photocopying, recording or otherwise, without the prior written permission of the publisher.

First Printing

U.S. Cataloguing in Publication Data
(Library of Congress Standards)

Raab, Evelyn.
    The clueless baker: baking from scratch—easy as pie / Evelyn Raab.—1st ed.
[216] p. : ill. ; cm.
Includes index.
Summary : A comprehensive introduction to the secrets of successful baking. Includes traditional and new recipes.
ISBN 1-55209-595-9 (pbk.)
1.Baking. 2. Bread. 3. Dessert. I. Title.
641.8/ 15 21 2001

Published in the United States in 2001 by
Firefly Books (U.S.) Inc.
P.O. Box 1338, Ellicott Station
Buffalo, New York, USA
14205

Published in Canada in 2001 by Key Porter Books Limited.

Illustrations: John Lightfoot
Design and electronic formatting: Jean Lightfoot Peters

Printed and bound in Canada

The Clueless Series™
™–Trademark of Key Porter Books,
used under licence by Firefly Books.

Dedication

For my husband George, an enthusiastic (but brutally honest) guinea pig, who wouldn't let me bake anything with cloves in it; and for my two intrepid sons, Dustin and Jared, who bravely struggled to try and keep up with the sheer volume of cookies that were produced during the writing of this book.

Contents

Acknowledgments

Thank you to Sarah Nashman for her meticulous proofreading and her uncanny ability to show up at our house at the precise moment that a batch of brownies was coming out of the oven.

Thanks to all my good friends who fearlessly tasted whatever I handed them—weird or wonderful—and helped me to decide which was which.

Thank you to my Mom who taught me that a person should always have a nice piece of cake in the house, and whose famous walnut strudel I am still trying to duplicate.

And a big thank you to my lovely chickens who not only generously provided me with endless eggs but also cheerfully polished off every last crumb of even my most spectacular baking disasters. The microwave cake included.

Getting Started

The oven looms before you. A darkened abyss. *The gates of hell.* You know—*you just know*—that whatever you put in there is doomed. Doomed and ruined. It will burn. Or collapse. Probably both.

Plus, your house will burn down...which is just as well, because after the mess you made of the kitchen it would take ten lifetimes to clean it up anyway. There is flour on the floor. Batter on the walls. Broken eggs in the sink (it was an accident). You're missing a spatula (you're praying it didn't get baked into the cake). The phone is ringing but you can't find it.

OK. Take a deep breath and relax. Help has arrived. Sort of.

What you need are some decent recipes, a good attitude and a plan. Baking can be—*should be*—fun. Also easy. It should be neither traumatic nor terrifying. And at the end of it, you should have something delicious to eat. Which will do wonders for your attitude, and is, after all, the point of the whole thing. Let's begin with the plan.

Baking—The Eleven-Step Program

1. *First decide what you want to make.* This should be easy. Do you feel like brownies or are you having a focaccia kind of day? Do you want to throw something together really fast, or do you feel like taking your time? Make up your mind, would you please?

2. *Choose a recipe.* This book is full of them.

3. *Read through the entire recipe.* Do you have all the ingredients you'll need? Are you sure? What about the baking pan? Do you have the right size? Will you need an electric mixer? Blender? Baking parchment? Does the dough have to *chill* before baking? *Rise? Meditate?* How long does it have to bake? Will whatever-it-is be ready to eat right away, or will you have to let it cool? It's all there in the recipe. If you just take the time to read it, you won't meet up with any, um, surprises.

4. *Preheat the oven.* Now. Before you do anything else. Go.

5. *Assemble the ingredients.* Take every single ingredient out and arrange them in a tasteful and attractive manner on your kitchen counter. If you are an obsessive-type person, you can even organize them in order of use.

6. *Prepare your baking pan.* Grease it and line it with parchment paper (if the recipe calls for it). Have some bowls ready; get out your mixer (find the beater thingies); grab a couple of spoons. You don't want to be groping around your junk drawer for a spatula when you're up to your elbows in batter.

7. *OK, now you can start.* Begin at the beginning, and follow the instructions *exactly.* This is no time to be creative. At least, not the first time. If you decide to bake the same thing again, you can be more adventurous—fiddle with the method and ingredients, if you want. But follow the directions at least once—you may even learn something.

8. *Keep your eye on the oven.* Set the timer and *make sure* you can hear it ring from wherever you'll be. If necessary, buy yourself a small portable oven timer that you can take out to the yard or down into the basement with you. I know you *think* you'll remember, but honestly—you won't. Not until you see smoke curling out the edges of the oven door. At which point it will be, alas, too late.

9. *Do the toothpick test* if the recipe suggests it. See page 28 for details.

10. *Ta da! Done.* Remove your delicious baked item(s) from the oven and carefully take it/them out of the baking pan(s). Let cool on a rack for as long as you can stand.

11. *Enjoy.* You earned it.

Bare Necessities, Electric Gizmos and Extra Added Widgets

Baking equipment tends to be pretty simple. You've got your pans, your bowls, your spatulas. Most of the things you really need are inexpensive and easy to find. If you're on a really tight budget, you can shop at secondhand stores and garage sales. If you recently inherited a fortune, you can blow it all at a fancy kitchenware store. Either way, your muffins will turn out just fine.

The Bare Necessities
Two 8 or 9-inch (20 or 22 cm) round cake pans
One 9 x 13-inch (22 x 33 cm) rectangular baking pan
One 8 or 9-inch (20 or 22 cm) square baking pan
Two 9 x 5-inch (23 x 13 cm) loaf pans
Two 10 x 15 inch (25 x 38 cm) cookie sheets with 1-inch (2 cm) sides (or similar size)
One muffin pan with 12 cups (or two with 6 cups each)
One 8 cup (2 liter) bundt pan (approximately 9 inches/23 cm diameter)

One 9 or 10-inch (23 or 25 cm) springform pan
One large or two smaller metal cooling racks
One set of "official" measuring spoons (imperial or metric or both)
One set of individual steel or plastic measuring cups (in graduated
   sizes of ¼, ⅓, ½ and 1 cup or metric equivalent)
Heatproof glass measuring cups (1 cup/250 mL and 4 cups/1 liter)
Mixing bowls (stainless steel or glass)—at least two really big ones
   (4 quarts/liters) and a couple of smaller ones (2 quarts/liters)
Whisk
Rubber scrapers (spatulas)
Wooden spoons
Flour sifter
Pastry blender (that chopper thingy for making pastry dough)
Pastry brush
Wooden rolling pin
Cookie cutters
Baking parchment paper or waxed paper

Electric Gizmos

Electric mixer—either handheld or on a stand
Blender
Food processor

Extra Added Widgets (for the more seriously motivated)

Pastry bag and decorating tips
One 10-inch (25 cm) tart pan with removable sides
One 10-inch (25 cm) tube pan (angel cake pan)
Mini-muffin pan

The Food Processor: What's It Good for Besides Shredding Cheese?

Yes, use your food processor to—

Cut shortening into dry ingredients when you're making pastry or biscuits

Combine butter, sugar and flour to make crumbly mixtures for topping pies or cakes

Cream together butter, sugar and eggs for cookies or cakes

Mix and knead yeast bread dough

Chop nuts

Slice apples or other fruit for pies

Shred carrots or apples for cakes or muffins

Uh, yeah, shred cheese

Grate chocolate—but not nicely

Puree bananas for cakes or muffins

Make graham cracker or chocolate cookie crumbs

No, don't try to use your food processor to—

Whip cream

Beat egg whites

Grate lemon or orange peel

Beat cake batter

Make a piña colada

The Essential Clueless Baking Cupboard

It's three in the morning. It suddenly occurs to you that life is not worth living without homemade chocolate chip cookies. Warm. Right now. Aren't you glad you keep this stuff in the house?

Absolute Necessities

All-purpose white flour
All-purpose whole wheat flour
Granulated white sugar
Brown sugar (*golden* brown, not dark brown)
Icing (or confectioners') sugar
Baking powder
Baking soda
Quick-rise instant yeast granules
Butter
Vegetable oil
Solid vegetable shortening
Eggs
Milk
Semisweet chocolate chips
Semisweet baking chocolate
Unsweetened baking chocolate
Unsweetened cocoa powder
Quick-cooking rolled oats (not instant)
Pure vanilla extract
Peanut butter
Cinnamon
Raisins
Walnuts
Non-stick baking spray

Noncompulsory Bonus Ingredients

Cake and pastry flour
Bread flour
Cornmeal
Graham cracker crumbs
Bran
Honey
Corn syrup
Molasses
Whipping cream
Sour cream
Buttermilk
Yogurt
Cream cheese
Cream of tartar
Ginger
Nutmeg
Pecans
Almonds
Hazelnuts
Dried cranberries
Dates
Coconut
Lemons

Emergency Substitutions

Can it be true? You've run out of chocolate? Baking powder? Don't panic, help is on the way. While not every ingredient can be replaced, the following substitutions may allow you to continue baking despite the missing whatever-it-is. In many cases, the finished product will be almost identical; however, some substitutions will result in a slightly different flavor or texture. Better, maybe. You never know.

1 oz unsweetened baking chocolate = 3 tbsp (45 mL) cocoa powder mixed with 1 tbsp (15 mL) vegetable oil or melted butter

1 oz (28 g) semisweet baking chocolate = 3 tbsp (45 mL) cocoa powder + 1 tbsp (15 mL) vegetable oil or melted butter + 1 tbsp (15 mL) sugar or/1 oz (28 g) unsweetened baking chocolate + 1 tbsp (15 mL) sugar or/3 tbsp (45 mL) semisweet chocolate chips

1 whole egg = 2 egg whites or/2 egg yolks + 1 tbsp (15 mL) water

1 cup (250 mL) vegetable oil = 1 cup (250 mL) butter or margarine or/1 cup (250 mL) solid vegetable shortening or/1 cup (250 mL) lard

1 tsp (5 mL) baking powder = ½ tsp (2 mL) cream of tartar + ¼ tsp (1 mL) baking soda

1 cup (250 mL) buttermilk = 1 cup (250 mL) plain yogurt or/1 tbsp (15 mL) lemon juice or vinegar + milk to equal 1 cup (250 mL)

1 cup (250 mL) sour cream = 3 tbsp (45 mL) butter + buttermilk or plain yogurt to equal 1 cup (250 mL)

1 cup (250 mL) brown sugar = 1 cup (250 mL) sugar + 2 tbsp (30 mL) molasses or/1 cup (250 mL) sugar (with no molasses, flavor will be different)

1 cup (250 mL) corn syrup = 1 ¼ cups (300 mL) sugar + ⅓ cup (75 mL) water and boiled until syrupy

1 cup (250 mL) honey = 1 ¼ cups (300 mL) sugar + ¼ cup (50 mL) liquid (water, milk or juice)

1 cup (250 mL) molasses = 1 cup (250 mL) honey or corn syrup (flavor will be different)

Don't cry over sour milk

In baking, sour milk is not gross. In fact, many recipes will use sour milk (or buttermilk or yogurt) to provide acidity in order for the baking soda to work properly. But most of us don't happen to have sour milk hanging around the house. So here's what you do:

Stir 1 tbsp (15 mL) vinegar or lemon juice into 1 cup (250 mL) milk and let it sit for at least 5 minutes. It will curdle and look disgusting. Congratulations, you are now the proud owner of some sour milk. You can use this in any recipe that calls for sour milk or buttermilk.

1 cup (250 mL) cake and pastry flour = 1 cup (250 mL) minus 2 tbsp (30 mL) all-purpose flour

1 tsp (5 mL) allspice = equal parts cinnamon, nutmeg and cloves to total 1 tsp (5 mL)

The Basics About Some Basics

What kind of sugar, exactly? How big an egg? How much salt? Here are a few additional details you'll need to know before you begin baking.

Eggs

Whenever eggs appear in a recipe, you should use standard, large eggs. White or brown or blue—choose whatever color matches your decor—it won't affect the taste, no matter what people have told you. Freshness counts—a fresh egg will separate more easily, and beat up lighter.

Butter

Yes, many of the recipes in this book contain butter. Because it tastes wonderful. And it bakes beautifully. And it's a more natural product than margarine. Unsalted butter is preferred for baking, since it allows you to control the amount of salt in the finished product. If, for whatever reason, you wish to avoid butter, you can substitute unsalted solid margarine for butter in any recipe. The results will be similar, but the flavor will be slightly different.

Margarine

When making frosting, sometimes it is easier to use unsalted soft margarine instead of butter. The flavor will not be as rich, but the texture will be creamier and fluffier. Your call.

Sugar

When a recipe calls for granulated sugar, it refers to regular, ordinary white sugar. It comes in paper bags. The usual stuff. If a recipe tells you to use brown sugar, it is referring to light brown or golden brown sugar—not dark brown. Although, if you like the more pronounced flavor of dark brown sugar, go ahead and use it instead of light brown. The recipe will work out fine.

Molasses

Molasses is a liquid sweetener, made from sugar cane (just like regular sugar). Depending on the process used to make it, molasses can range in color from medium brown to jet black. Generally speaking, the darker the color, the stronger the taste. But even a light molasses will have a distinctive flavor. So if you like it, use it. If not, then substitute another liquid sweetener—like honey or corn syrup. It will bake just fine.

Salt

Most of the sweet recipes in this book *do not* contain salt in the ingredients. If you wish, you may to add a pinch (but *just* a pinch!) to the batter or dough, as long as the recipe doesn't already call for it.

Whipping Cream

Depending on where you live, whipping cream may be called by a variety of names: heavy cream, double cream, even 35% cream. The important thing is that the cream contains about 35% butterfat so that it will whip properly. This information will appear somewhere on the carton. If you're not planning to whip the cream, the butterfat content isn't as critical—and you can substitute a lower fat cream, if you prefer.

Flour—Is Nothing Ever Simple?

You're definitely going to need flour. But what kind of flour? Or didn't you know you had a choice?

Most baking recipes use wheat flour. It is made (surprise) from wheat grain, and comes in several different types. Each type of wheat flour is best suited for a specific purpose. Here goes:

Bleached white flour is the most widely available kind of flour. It's the stuff you get in bags at the supermarket, and is sold under various brand names. If the bag says nothing else (like unbleached or whole wheat) you can be sure it's bleached white flour. This product has been milled, the bran sifted out, and then bleached by chemical means to make it dazzlingly white. Vitamins and whatnot have been added to put back some of the nutrients that were removed during the refining process. *All-purpose white flour* can be used for most baking purposes, unless the recipe specifies another type of flour. Wheat flour is also available as a *cake and pastry flour* (which is best for light cakes and pastries) and *bread flour* (which is best for, oh, you know...).

Unbleached white flour is basically the same as bleached white flour, except that it, well, hasn't been bleached and so remains a creamy white color. *All-purpose unbleached white flour* can be used in any recipe that calls for all-purpose flour. In fact, many people prefer to use it because it has undergone less processing than bleached flour. *Unbleached bread flour* is great for bread-baking, and of course, *unbleached cake and pastry flour* is good for, well, cakes and pastries.

Whole wheat flour is made from ground-up kernels of wheat. Period. Nothing is taken out. The outside layer of bran and the wheat germ are both left in the flour, giving it a darker color, a more pronounced flavor and a coarser texture than white flour. It contains all the nutrients found in wheat and provides a hefty dose of fibre too. So why don't we use it all the time? Well, mostly because whole wheat flour will produce a baked product that is heavier than what you may be accustomed to, and it is too coarse to use in delicate cakes and pastries. If you want to experiment with whole wheat flour, try replacing a small proportion of the white flour in a recipe with whole wheat flour and see how it turns out. If you like the results, you can try a little more next time. Use *all-purpose whole wheat flour* for general baking, *whole wheat bread flour* for baking bread, and *whole wheat pastry flour* for cakes and pastries. Whole wheat flour should be kept refrigerated (or bought in smaller quantities more frequently) because it doesn't keep as well as white flour.

Gluten

Gluten is a stretchy protein that is found in wheat flour (as well as some other grains, like oats and rye). This is what gives bread its spongy texture and allows a loaf of bread to hold itself up as it rises. When we knead the dough, we are developing the gluten structure, and causing the fibers to stretch and strengthen. This is a good thing in bread, and so a high gluten content flour—also known as a "hard" flour—is best for that purpose. All of the bread recipes in this book can be made with all-purpose flour, but a high gluten "hard" bread flour will give you an even better result.

Cake and pastry flour is a low-gluten flour and is best for baking more delicate things—like pastries and light cakes. After all, you don't want to have to gnaw through gluten when you're eating chocolate cake or a slice of apple pie. You want your cakes and pastries to be fluffy and fragile.

And finally, where would we be without compromise? That's where all-purpose flour comes in. Not as "hard" as bread flour, and not as "soft" as pastry flour, it has enough gluten to make a decent loaf of bread, but can also be used to bake cakes and pastries.

Most of the recipes in this book call for all-purpose flour, but a few do specify cake and pastry flour so read the recipes carefully.

Chocolate. Need We Say More?

Well, yes, actually. We need to say lots more. Because you need to know this stuff.

Chocolate is made from the fruit of a tropical bush. You pick the beans, whack off their shells, roast them and then squeeze out the juice. From that, eventually, chocolate is made. The juice, which is technically called *cocoa liquor*, contains both the cocoa solids (the chocolate-flavored part) and cocoa butter (the creamy smooth melt-in-your-mouth part). These two substances are combined in different proportions, with varying amounts of sugar, to make your basic hunk of chocolate.

Unsweetened chocolate is a mixture of cocoa solids and cocoa butter. No sugar. It has an intense chocolate flavor and is often used in baking when you're looking for a big chocolate hit without added sweetness. Most likely, you will buy it in a package of eight 1-oz (28 gram) squares. Anyone who has accidentally taken a bite of unsweetened baking chocolate will probably not want to do that ever again.

Semisweet (or bittersweet) chocolate comprises cocoa solids mixed with cocoa butter and sugar (and sometimes other ingredients, like vanilla). Semisweet chocolate contains more sugar than bittersweet chocolate, but they're both deliciously edible, and are generally interchangeable in recipes. Semisweet chocolate is commonly sold in packages of eight 1-oz (28 gram) squares, as well as in large and small bars meant for snacking. It's sometimes more economical to buy a big bar of good quality eating chocolate than a package of baking chocolate squares (but you'll need an accurate kitchen scale to measure the right amount for your recipe).

Chocolate chips are usually made from semisweet chocolate and are formulated to hold their shape when baked in a cookie or cake. But otherwise, semisweet chocolate chips can usually be substituted—*weight for weight*—for semisweet baking chocolate in recipes where the chocolate is melted. See page 17 for a somewhat imprecise guide to using chocolate chips in place of semisweet baking chocolate.

Milk chocolate is made by taking some semisweet chocolate, adding a little milk and a bit more sugar, and—ta da—that wonderfully sweet taste. Mostly munched in the form of chocolate bars, milk chocolate can occasionally be used in baking. But not often. The flavor is mild and creamy and quite sweet, so it doesn't pack a really big chocolate wallop. But still. You've got to love it because, after all, it *is* chocolate.

White chocolate is essentially just cocoa butter mixed with sugar and a few other odds and ends. The cocoa solids (the brown substance that tastes like chocolate) have been left out of the picture. A good white chocolate tastes rich and creamy, and is often used in cheesecakes or melted to drizzle onto cookies or cakes. It also comes in a chip form, which can be added to your favorite chocolate chip recipe in place of part or all of the semisweet chocolate chips. In regular baking, however, don't try to substitute it for any other type of chocolate. It's a different animal altogether.

Unsweetened cocoa powder is made by taking your cocoa solids and grinding them up to a powder. No sugar, no cocoa butter, no nothing. It is used extensively in baking to add a serious chocolate punch, with no additional fat or sweetness. Very handy. It's easy to use, since it can often be mixed with the dry ingredients in a recipe. Unsweetened cocoa powder can also be substituted for unsweetened baking chocolate, as long as you add some shortening to take the place of the missing cocoa butter (see page 17).

Baking Fundamentals: Simple Answers to Profound Questions

It's all fine and dandy to talk about separating an egg—but from what? And how? And what about sifting? Do we really have to do that? What's it all about, anyway? Oh, take it easy. All the answers are right here.

Is there an easy way to measure butter?

Measuring solid butter is a messy and unsatisfying business. It's difficult to pack the butter solidly into your measuring cup to make sure you have exactly the right amount. What you need is a shortcut.

Let's say the recipe calls for ½ cup (125 mL) of butter. So…fill a measuring cup with cold (!) water to the ½ cup (125 mL) level, then add chunks of butter to the measuring cup until the water reaches the 1 cup (250 mL) level. Pour off all the water and, ta da! You have ½ cup (125 mL) butter.

Oh, and by the way, this method works just as well with any solid fat such as margarine, lard or vegetable shortening.

How do I separate an egg?

If you've never done this before, practice your egg-separating technique at an uncrucial moment—say, when you're making scrambled eggs or something. Not when you are about to make your first angel food cake. In order for egg whites to beat properly, there can be not a smidgen—not an iota, not a subatomic particle—of egg yolk mixed into them. So you'll have to be very careful, won't you?

Have three bowls ready—two large ones and a small one. Crack the egg by tapping it firmly against the side of one bowl. Using both hands, carefully pry the two halves apart and, holding the yolk back, let the white part drain into the small bowl. Gently transfer the yolk back and forth between the two half shells, letting as much of the white drip down into the *small* bowl as possible. Now, dump the yolk into one of the large bowls, and pour the white from the small bowl into the other large bowl. Repeat the process with the remaining eggs.

Now…why did we drain the egg white into a small bowl first? This is so that if you have already successfully separated five eggs, and number six explodes on cracking and contaminates the white, you have only ruined *one* egg—not six. Simply put the mucked-up egg aside to use in another recipe (or scramble it for lunch) and proceed with a new egg.

Bonus cheater's trick: Crack your egg into a funnel set over a bowl. The white should drain through the funnel tube, leaving the yolk high and dry.

How do I beat egg whites?

Seems impossible, doesn't it? That gloppy egg white should turn into such lovely, puffy meringue? Well it's not impossible—it's not even difficult.

Let your separated egg whites come to room temperature in a large, *scrupulously* clean bowl. (Cold eggs separate more easily, but room temperature eggs beat up fluffier.) Using an electric beater on high speed, beat the egg whites until foamy, scraping down the sides of the bowl a few times with a rubber scraper. If your recipe calls for sugar to be added to the egg whites, begin to add it gradually—a few spoonfuls at a time. This will allow the sugar to be slowly absorbed by the egg whites. Continue beating constantly at high speed until the egg whites are thick and white and glossy.

If you can't tell if your egg whites are whipped enough, stop beating and lift the beaters from the bowl. If the meringue stands upright in a glossy peak without collapsing, it's done.

If you are beating without sugar, the meringue will be more fragile and less glossy. Be sure you don't overbeat it, because it will collapse into a pathetic mess and be useless. Better underbeat than overbeat.

Flour: To sift or not to sift...that is the question.

You're thinking: "Awwww—do I have to?"

The answer is a definite maybe. The whole point of sifting flour is to remove lumps, and to make it light and fluffy. When you buy a bag of flour, it has already been sifted so you're not likely to find any lumps in it. However, if it has been sitting on the shelf for quite a while, it may have settled and become compressed—no longer as light and fluffy as it should be. So should you sift it? Sometimes.

Yes, sift:
- If you are making a cake where a light and fluffy texture is especially important
- If you can actually *see* lumps in the flour
- If you want to evenly combine, for instance, cocoa powder or spices with flour
- If you feel like it (it'll never do any harm)

No, don't bother:
- If you're making bread
- If you're making a moist, heavy cake or muffins
- If you're making cookies

Can't you be more specific about the amount of flour in a bread recipe?

Well no, actually. You probably wouldn't notice it, but different flours contain different amounts of moisture. This may not be obvious in stuff like cookies or cakes, but for some reason it makes a big difference when you're baking a yeast bread. One type of flour might absorb a lot more liquid than another type—causing the dough to be heavier and drier, or softer and stickier.

Most yeast bread recipes will tell you to add flour gradually, a bit at a time, until it reaches the right texture. And that's just what you should do. Begin with the least amount of flour specified in the recipe, and continue adding until the dough is smooth and elastic. You may not need the entire amount of flour that the recipe suggests, or you may need a bit more than it requires.

Sorry that's as specific as it gets. Bread baking is art—not nuclear physics.

Oven temperature—how can we be sure?

In the bad old days, when your great-grandma baked a loaf of bread in her big old woodstove, she probably just stuck her hand into the oven and could tell right away if it was hot enough. Fortunately for us, it is no longer necessary to risk second-degree burns just to bake a cake. We set the temperature on the oven and never give it another thought. But can we trust it? Maybe not.

Occasionally an oven will lie. So how do you know?

Well, your first clue would be when your chocolate chip cookies burst into flames. But that is an extreme example. Most of the time, the temperature will be just a little bit off. Your recipes will brown too quickly, or the outsides will be done before the insides are fully baked. The bottoms of cakes or cookies may burn, or your pie crust may turn brown before the filling is cooked.

If you suspect that you're the victim of oven temperature fraud, buy yourself an inexpensive oven thermometer and use it to check. That way you can adjust the setting on your oven dial to compensate for the inaccuracy.

Or, if all else fails, you can call Great-grandma. She'll know what to do.

What's it all about, anyway?

Cookies. It's all about cookies.

Quick Breads and Yeast Breads

Is there anything more straightforward, more honest, than a loaf of bread? Real bread. Made with actual flour, mixed and kneaded with your very own hands. Woven into a braid, or squashed into a loaf pan, sprinkled with seeds or glazed with egg yolk, served warm. With butter. Go ahead—have a slice. You know you can't resist.

Quick Breads
Beer Bread

The famous toothpick test

Relax, you don't have to study for this. The toothpick test is a simple way of finding out whether the cake or bread you're baking is ready to come out of the oven. Here's what you do:

Open the oven door and, without removing the pan from the rack, take a clean toothpick and stick it into the cake, close to the middle. If the cake is done, the toothpick will be clean when you pull it out, with no batter clinging to it. If the cake needs to bake a little longer, it will be coated with cake batter. Slide the pan back into the oven and give it another 5 minutes, then test again. Repeat until your cake passes the test.

You couldn't bring yourself to throw it out, could you—that bottle of beer at the back of the fridge, the one that's been there for two weeks? Now you don't have to. This delicious bread is best served warm.

3 cups	750 mL	all-purpose flour
3 tbsp	45 mL	granulated sugar
1 tbsp	15 mL	baking powder
1 tsp	5 mL	salt
½ tsp	2 mL	baking soda
1 bottle		(12 oz/342 mL) beer, flat is fine (fizzy is fine too)
		Optional ingredients: poppy seeds, sesame seeds, caraway seeds, chopped sun-dried tomatoes, chopped olives, crumbled herbs

Preheat the oven to 375° F (190° C).

In a large bowl, stir together the flour, sugar, baking powder, salt and baking soda. Add the beer and any optional ingredients you like, and stir until thoroughly mixed into a gluey batter. Dump batter into a greased 9 x 5-inch (23 x 13 cm) loaf pan and bake for 45 to 50 minutes—until golden brown on top and no longer gooey in the center (do the toothpick test, see sidebar).

Remove from pan and serve warm, or let cool on a rack and serve later. Whatever.

Makes one unbelievably easy loaf of bread.

The Clueless Baker

Great Pumpkin Bread

Make this loaf with canned pumpkin (the kind you use for pies) or with your own homemade pumpkin puree (see page 183). You can even use leftover mashed squash, if you happen to have some in the fridge.

1 ½ cups	375 mL	granulated sugar
½ cup	125 mL	vegetable oil
2		eggs
1 cup	250 mL	canned (or homemade) pumpkin puree
1 ½ cups	375 mL	all-purpose flour
½ tsp	2 mL	cinnamon
½ tsp	2 mL	nutmeg
½ tsp	2 mL	baking soda
½ tsp	2 mL	baking powder
½ cup	125 mL	chopped walnuts (optional)

Preheat the oven to 350° F (180° C).

In a large bowl, beat together the sugar, oil and eggs with an electric mixer until well blended—about 2 to 3 minutes. Add the pumpkin puree and beat for another minute or two.

In another bowl, mix together the flour, cinnamon, nutmeg, baking soda and baking powder. Add this to the pumpkin mixture, in 2 or 3 additions, beating well after each addition. Stir in the walnuts if you're using them.

Spoon the batter into a well-greased 9 x 5-inch (23 x 13 cm) loaf pan and bake for about 1 hour and 15 minutes, or until a toothpick stuck into the middle of the loaf comes out clean. Let cool in the baking pan for about 10 minutes, then remove from pan and cool completely on a wire rack.

Makes one heartwarming 9 x 5-inch (23 x 13 cm) loaf.

Ridiculously Easy Cheese Bread

A bowl of homemade soup, a green salad. A loaf of this bread. There. Dinner.

2 cups	500 mL	all-purpose flour
4 tsp	20 mL	baking powder
1 tbsp	15 mL	granulated sugar
½ tsp	2 mL	dry mustard powder
½ tsp	2 mL	salt
1 ¼ cups	300 mL	shredded cheese (sharp cheddar, Monterey jack, Swiss—actually anything except processed cheese)
1		egg
1 cup	250 mL	milk
2 tbsp	15 mL	vegetable oil

Preheat the oven to 375° F (190° C).

In a large bowl, stir together the flour, baking powder, sugar, mustard powder and salt until thoroughly combined. Dump in the shredded cheese and toss until mixed.

In a smaller bowl, beat the egg with the milk and the vegetable oil. Pour the entire egg mixture into the flour mixture and stir just until all the ingredients are moistened. The batter will be lumpy—but that's OK.

Spoon batter into a greased 9 x 5-inch (23 x 13 cm) loaf pan and bake for 35 to 40 minutes—or until the top is lightly browned. Allow bread to cool for about 10 minutes before attempting to remove from the pan.

Makes one ridiculously easy but totally cheesy loaf.

Variation

Add chopped jalapeño peppers, onions, olives or sun-dried tomatoes to the batter when you add the cheese. Or stir some coarsely ground black pepper, crushed red pepper flakes, oregano or rosemary into the flour mixture.

Cranberry Irish Soda Bread

This bread is at its best when served warm, straight from the oven, with plenty of butter. But in the (highly unlikely) event that there is any left over, it makes great breakfast toast the next day.

3 ¾ cups	850 mL	all-purpose flour
¼ cup	50 mL	light brown sugar
1 ½ tbsp	22 mL	baking powder
½ tsp	1 mL	baking soda
1 tsp	5 mL	salt
¾ cup	175 mL	dried cranberries, chopped (or raisins or dried currants)
2 cups	500 mL	buttermilk
1		egg

Preheat the oven to 375° F (190° C).

In a large bowl, mix together the flour, brown sugar, baking powder, baking soda and salt. Add the dried cranberries and mix well.

In another bowl, stir together the buttermilk and the egg. Pour the buttermilk mixture into the flour mixture, and stir well until everything is blended. The dough will be pretty soft—that's OK. Sprinkle some additional flour onto the counter or table (or wherever you like to work) and turn the dough out onto this floured surface. Knead the dough about 10 times—just to make it smooth-ish and pliable.

Gently form it into one large round loaf and place it on a well-greased baking sheet. With a very sharp knife, cut a shallow X into the top of the loaf. This will allow the loaf to expand in a tasteful and attractive manner in the oven, rather than splitting weirdly.

Bake for 55 to 60 minutes, or until the loaf is nicely browned and a toothpick poked into the middle comes out clean.

Makes one large round loaf.

Unpretentious Zucchini Bread

A bit of lime helps poor, humble zucchini find true personal fulfill-ment. If only it were this easy for the rest of us.

2 cups	500 mL	all-purpose flour
¾ cup	175 mL	light brown sugar
2 tsp	10 mL	baking powder
½ tsp	2 mL	baking soda
½ cup	125 mL	vegetable oil
¼ cup	50 mL	milk
1		egg
1 ½ cups	375 mL	coarsely grated zucchini (about 2 smallish ones)
½ cup	125 mL	chopped walnuts
		Grated rind of one lime or lemon

Preheat the oven to 350° F (180° C).

In a large bowl, mix together the flour, brown sugar, baking powder and baking soda.

In another bowl, beat together the vegetable oil, milk and egg.

Add the egg mixture to the flour mixture, and stir until the ingredients are just moistened. Now stir in the zucchini, walnuts and lime or lemon rind, mixing until everything is evenly distributed in the batter. (This is a very thick batter—but that's OK. The grated zucchini will release additional moisture as it bakes.)

Dump into a well-greased 9 x 5-inch (23 x 13 cm) loaf pan and bake for 55 to 60 minutes, or until the top is golden brown and it passes the toothpick test (see page 28).

Remove loaf from the baking pan and let cool completely before slicing. If you can possibly resist eating it immediately, it actually improves if you wrap it in foil and let it sit overnight.

Makes one 9 x 5-inch (23 x 13 cm) unpretentious loaf.

Blender Banana Bread

Hey—look. There. Beside the microwave. Under the oranges. Aren't those a couple of mushy old bananas? Yes! It's banana bread time.

1 ¼ cups	300 mL	all-purpose flour
1 cup	250 mL	granulated sugar
1 tsp	5 mL	baking soda
½ cup	125 mL	vegetable oil
2		seriously ripe bananas
2		eggs

Preheat the oven to 350° F (180° C).

In a large bowl, stir together the flour, sugar and baking soda.

Put the oil, bananas and eggs into the container of a blender and blend to a smooth goo. Pour the banana mixture into the flour mixture, and stir until thoroughly combined.

Spoon the batter into a well-greased 9 x 5-inch (23 x 13 cm) loaf pan, and bake for about an hour, or until a toothpick poked into the middle of the loaf comes out clean. Remove from the pan and place on a rack to cool.

Makes one simply superb loaf of banana bread.

Extra extra!

Want to throw in some chopped nuts? Chocolate chips? Raisins? Go ahead! It'll be just fine. Add about ¾ cup (175 mL) of any one (or combination) of the above to the batter when you combine the wet and dry ingredients. It's your banana bread now, baby.

Cranberry Orange Bread

Painless nut chopping

Painless for you, that is.

Measure your walnuts, pecans, almonds or hazelnuts into a zip-top plastic bag. Roll with a rolling pin until the nuts are chopped the way you want them. Ta da!

A lovely thing to serve, thinly sliced, at your next tea party. Not planning a tea party? Pity.

2 cups	500 mL	all-purpose flour
1 cup	250 mL	granulated sugar
1 ½ tsp	7 mL	baking powder
½ tsp	2 mL	baking soda
1		medium orange (juice squeezed and zest grated)
1		egg
¼ cup	50 mL	vegetable oil
1 cup	250 mL	fresh (or frozen) cranberries, quartered
½ cup	125 mL	chopped walnuts

Preheat the oven to 350° F (180° C).

In a large bowl, mix together the flour, sugar, baking powder and baking soda. Squeeze the juice from the orange into a measuring cup, and add just enough water to it to measure ¾ cup (175 mL) of liquid. Pour this into a small bowl, and beat together with the grated zest, the egg and the vegetable oil.

Add the juice mixture to the flour mixture, and stir until everything is moistened. Dump in the cranberries and walnuts, and continue to stir just until the batter is evenly mixed. (Don't overmix.) Scoop batter into a well-greased 9 x 5-inch (23 x 13 cm) loaf pan and bake for 55 to 60 minutes, or until the top is golden brown and it passes the toothpick test (see page 28).

Remove loaf from the baking pan and let cool completely on a wire rack before slicing. In fact, this tastes even better if you wrap it in foil and let it sit overnight. No, really.

Makes one 9 x 5-inch (23 x 13 cm) loaf.

Blueberry Lemon Bread

You've invited Great-aunt Gertrude to lunch. What on earth are you going to serve? Well, tuna casserole, of course. And this, with her tea. She'll be so impressed.

Bread

1 ½ cups	375 mL	all-purpose flour
2 tsp	10 mL	baking powder
1		lemon, zest grated
1 cup	250 mL	granulated sugar
⅓ cup	75 mL	butter, softened
2		eggs
½ cup	125 mL	milk
1 cup	250 mL	blueberries, fresh or frozen (don't thaw them!)

Lemon syrup

1		lemon, juice squeezed
⅓ cup	75 mL	granulated sugar

Preheat the oven to 350° F (180° C).

In a bowl, stir together the flour and the baking powder. Set aside.

Grate the zest from the lemon into a small bowl and squeeze the juice into another bowl. Set these aside too.

In a large mixing bowl, beat the sugar and the butter with an electric mixer until fluffy. Add the eggs, one at a time, beating well after each. Beat in the grated lemon zest. Now, add the flour mixture in 2 or 3 additions, alternating with the milk, beating until the batter is smooth. Quickly fold in the blueberries until they're evenly distributed. Too much mixing will leave you with blue batter—not fatal, just weird looking.

Pour batter into a well-greased 9 x 5-inch (23 x 13 cm) loaf pan and bake for 60 to 70 minutes, until the top is golden brown and a toothpick poked into the middle comes out clean. Don't remove it from the pan yet!

Now make the lemon syrup. Combine the reserved lemon juice with the ⅓ cup (75 mL) of sugar, and heat it in a small saucepan or in the microwave, just until the sugar dissolves and the mixture is hot.

Grate first, squeeze later

Whenever a recipe calls for both the grated zest (this is the *yellow* part of the lemon zest) *and* the juice of a lemon, always grate first, then squeeze afterwards. Doesn't that just make sense?

With a toothpick, poke holes all over the top of the loaf and spoon the syrup over, allowing it to soak in. Let cool in the pan for 30 minutes before removing to a rack to cool completely.

Makes one refreshingly lemony 9 x 5-inch (23 x 13 cm) loaf.

Grease Is Not a Four-Letter Word

It's happened to all of us. The cookies that refuse to leave the cookie sheet. The cake (or worse—half of a cake) that refuses to exit the baking pan. The otherwise perfect loaf of bread that stubbornly resists all attempts to pry it loose.

It's your fault. If you'd used the spray stuff, everything would have turned out just fine.

Non-stick cooking spray is a perfectly innocent product made from a combination of vegetable oil, lecithin and environmentally friendly propellants. It's more effective than anything else at keeping baked stuff from sticking to the pan. It's also very easy to use.

The down side is that non-stick cooking spray comes packaged in a big, clunky, non-reusable, probably non-recyclable spray can that creates garbage. Unfortunate. But at least you'll have a beautiful cake as consolation.

Date-Nut Bread in a Can

You can bake this recipe in two regular loaf pans, if you don't feel like messing around with the cans. But it won't be nearly as much fun.

1 ½ cups	375 mL	chopped, pitted dates
1 tsp	5 mL	baking soda
1 cup	250 mL	boiling water
1 cup	250 mL	granulated sugar
1		egg
2 cups	500 mL	all-purpose flour
1 tsp	5 mL	baking powder
1 tsp	5 mL	vanilla
½ cup	125 mL	chopped walnuts
4		empty 10-oz (284 g) soup (or whatever) cans

Preheat the oven to 325° F (160° C).

Prepare the four empty cans, by washing them thoroughly (be careful of the sharp edges), and greasing them well with non-stick spray or shortening.

Measure the chopped dates into a large mixing bowl, and toss with the baking soda. Pour in the boiling water, stir well, then let the mixture sit until cool, about 30 minutes.

Once the date mixture is cool, add the sugar, egg, flour, baking powder and vanilla and mix well. Stir in the chopped walnuts. Pour in the batter into the prepared cans, filling them equally. Place cans on a baking sheet and bake for 35 to 40 minutes, or until a toothpick poked in the center of the bread comes out clean.

Remove breads from the cans, and let cool completely. If you have trouble getting the bread out, turn it over, remove the bottom with a can opener, and push the bread out from below.

Makes four nifty little round breads, perfect for tea party sandwiches (with cream cheese, please) or to give as gifts.

Chopping dates (or, for that matter, raisins or dried apricots or anything else like that)

This is a thankless, sticky task. So here's a way to make it easier.

Toss the dates with a little of the flour from the recipe until well coated. Then, using a pair of scissors, snip them into pieces.

And if you borrowed the scissors from the family sewing kit, don't forget to wash them before returning them. Oh—and don't forget to return them.

Crummy Apple Bread

But what kind of apples?

Whenever using apples in a baking recipe, you can use almost any type of apple you might happen to have in the house—McIntosh, Cortland, Empire, Rome, Jonathan, Spy. The only kinds of apples that really don't work well in baking are Red or Yellow Delicious. Save those for your lunchbox.

Make this crumble-topped loaf on a cold fall afternoon. Not only does it taste delicious, but it will make your house smell great. Bonus.

2 cups	500 mL	all-purpose flour
2 tsp	10 mL	baking powder
½ tsp	2 mL	baking soda
1 cup	250 mL	granulated sugar
½ cup	125 mL	vegetable oil
2		eggs
2 tsp	10 mL	vanilla
2 cups	500 mL	peeled, chopped apples (about 3 medium apples)
½ cup	125 mL	chopped walnuts
¼ cup	50 mL	All-Purpose Crumble Topping (see page 176)

Preheat the oven to 350° F (180° C).

In a large mixing bowl, stir together the flour, baking powder and baking soda. Set aside.

In the container of a blender or food processor, combine the sugar, vegetable oil, eggs and vanilla. Blend for a minute or two, scraping down the sides once or twice, until the mixture is smooth. Add this to the flour mixture, and stir until the dry ingredients are smoothly combined. Dump in the chopped apples and walnuts, and stir to just mix.

Pour batter into a well-greased 9 x 5-inch (23 x 13 cm) loaf pan and sprinkle evenly with the crumble topping mixture. Bake for 60 to 70 minutes, until the crumbly topping is golden brown and the loaf passes the toothpick test (see page 28). Remove bread from the pan and let cool completely on a wire rack before slicing.

Makes one crummy 9 x 5-inch (23 x 13 cm) loaf.

Yeast Breads

No-Knead Casserole Bread

Let's start with something simple, shall we? This one requires no finicky kneading (is that the part that scares you?) and can easily be varied to suit your mood.

3 ½ cups	875 mL	all-purpose flour, divided
4 ½ tsp	22 mL	(2 envelopes) quick-rise instant yeast
3 tbsp	45 mL	granulated sugar
1 tsp	5 mL	salt
¾ cup	175 mL	water
1 cup	250 mL	milk
¼ cup	50 mL	butter
1		egg

In a large mixing bowl, stir together 2 cups (500 mL) of the flour (pay attention—this is only *part* of the flour, y'hear?) the yeast, sugar and salt.

In a saucepan over low heat or in a microwave-safe bowl in the microwave, heat the water, milk and butter until it is just a little uncomfortably warm. Add it to the flour mixture. Beat with an electric mixer (or stir by hand with a wooden spoon) for a few minutes, until the texture is quite gooey. Then beat in the egg and the remaining flour, and beat or stir until the mixture is sticky and difficult to stir. Cover the bowl with plastic wrap, and place it in a warm spot to rise (see Getting a Rise Out of Your Dough, page 40) until doubled in volume—30 to 45 minutes.

With a wooden spoon, stir down the batter to deflate it. Dump into a well-greased 2-quart (2 liter) casserole dish and let rise again, until *not quite* double in volume—15 to 20 minutes.

Meanwhile, preheat the oven to 350° F (180° C).

Place the casserole dish in the oven and bake for 40 to 45 minutes, or until the bread is golden brown on top and sounds hollow when you tap it with your finger.

Makes one large loaf.

Mood Bread—Choose Your Variation

Whole Wheat Casserole Bread

Substitute 1 to 1 ½ cups (250 to 375 mL) whole wheat flour for the same quantity of all-purpose flour in the recipe. Bake the same as for the basic bread (or combine with one of the following variations).

Raisin Casserole Bread

Stir 1 cup (250 mL) raisins into the batter just before the first rise. Bake the same as for the basic bread.

Cheese Casserole Bread

Reduce the butter to 2 tbsp (30 mL). Add 1 ½ cups (375 mL) grated sharp cheddar cheese to the batter when you beat in the egg. Bake the same as for the basic bread.

Feta and Olive Casserole Bread

Substitute olive oil for the butter in the basic recipe. Stir 1 cup (250 mL) pitted black olives (preferably kalamata or other brine-cured ones) into the batter just before the first rise. Sprinkle the top of the bread with ½ cup (125 mL) crumbled feta cheese just before the second rise. Bake the same as for the basic bread.

Getting a Rise Out of Your Dough

Fine. You've made the dough. Now where do you put it to rise? Here are some ideas:

- Fill a large pan or bowl with hot tap water and place it in the bottom of your oven. *Do not turn the oven on.* Place your dough in a bowl on a rack over the hot water and close the oven door. The water will add both warmth and humidity to the oven—a perfect environment for yeast dough.
- If you have a microwave, fill a measuring cup with water and place it in the microwave. Zap until it comes to a boil, then shove it into a corner of the microwave. Put your bowl of dough in and close the door. Same deal—warmth and humidity.
- Cover your dough with plastic wrap (to keep the surface from drying out) and place the bowl on top of your refrigerator. It's a lovely warm spot for dough to rise.

Wonderful White Bread

This is white bread you don't have to feel guilty about.

6 cups	1500 mL	all-purpose flour *(approximately)*, divided
3 tbsp	45 mL	granulated sugar
4 ½ tsp	22 mL	(2 envelopes) quick-rise instant yeast
2 tsp	10 mL	salt
1 ½ cups	375 mL	water
½ cup	125 mL	milk
2 tbsp	30 mL	vegetable oil

In a large bowl, stir together 2 (500 mL) cups of the flour, the sugar, yeast and salt.

Mix together the water, milk and vegetable oil and heat—in the microwave or in a saucepan on the stove—until very warm but not boiling. Add this to the flour mixture, stirring to make a yucky batter. Add the remaining flour, one cup at a time, until the mixture becomes a soft sticky dough that is difficult to stir. Dump it out onto a floured surface and knead by hand, sprinkling with flour whenever necessary, until it is smooth and elastic and no longer sticky. This should take about 8 to 10 minutes. *(You might not have to use all the flour.)*

Place the dough in an oiled bowl, and turn it over to oil the top of the dough. Cover with a damp towel or plastic wrap and place in a warm spot to rise until doubled in size—about 30 to 45 minutes (see page 40).

When the dough has risen to about double the size, punch it down, then knead it a few times on a floured surface. Let the dough rest while you grease the baking pans, then form it into two loaves (see page 47) and place them into the pans to rise again—this time to almost (not quite) double—for about 30 minutes.

Preheat the oven to 400° F (200° C).

Bake loaves for 25 to 30 minutes, or until they're nicely browned on top and sound hollow when you tap them. Remove from pans and don't you dare taste them until completely cool. Ha. Like you could resist.

Makes 2 gorgeous loaves of bread.

Variation

Wonderful Whole Wheat Substitute 2 cups (500 mL) of whole wheat flour for 2 cups (500 mL) of the all-purpose flour in the recipe. The resulting bread will be slightly more dense, but still wonderful.

100% Whole Wheat Bread

This whole wheat bread is neither overly dense nor annoyingly healthy tasting. It's just delicious. And, well, good for you.

8 ½ cups	2 liters	whole wheat flour *(approximately)*, divided
4 ½ tsp	22 mL	(2 envelopes) quick-rise instant yeast
2 ½ tsp	12 mL	salt
1 ½ cups	375 mL	water
1 ½ cups	375 mL	milk
¼ cup	50 mL	honey (or maple syrup, molasses or corn syrup)
¼ cup	50 mL	vegetable oil

In a large mixing bowl, stir together 4 cups (1 liter) of the flour (note: this is only *part* of the flour—pay attention), the yeast and salt.

In a small saucepan or heatproof measuring cup, mix together the water, milk, honey (or whatever) and vegetable oil. Heat over low heat until it's just uncomfortably warm to the touch, then add it to the flour mixture. Using an electric mixer, beat for 2 minutes on high speed, until a gooey but smooth dough forms. Now, stirring with a wooden spoon, add the remaining flour, ½ cup (125 mL) at a time, until the dough becomes too difficult to stir. Turn the dough out onto a well-floured surface, and knead by hand (see page 46) until smooth and elastic, adding additional flour to keep it from sticking to either your hands or the table—about 6 to 8 minutes. (*You might not have to use all the flour.*) When the dough feels just damp—not sticky—and feels like your earlobe when you pinch it, it's done.

Place the dough in a large oiled bowl, turning it over to oil the top of the dough. Cover with plastic wrap and place it in a warm spot to rise (see page 40) until doubled—about 30 to 45 minutes.

Once the dough has risen, make a fist and punch it down to deflate it. Turn it out onto the table (or wherever you do your kneading) and knead it a few times. Cut the dough in half. Form the dough into two loaves, using any shaping method you like (see page 47). Place in well-greased baking pans or sheets, cover, and let rise again, until not quite double—about 30 minutes.

Meanwhile, preheat the oven to 375° F (190° C).

Bake for 35 to 40 minutes, until loaves are golden brown and sound hollow when you tap them with your finger. Let cool on a rack. If you can make yourself wait that long.

Makes two medium loaves.

Yeast—A Matter of Life or Death

Up until now, the subject of baking has been a relatively simple matter. You mix some stuff, put it in a pan, bake it. Pretty straightforward.

With yeast, it gets a bit weird.

Yeast is no mere ingredient. It is a living organism. Like a hamster, it requires care and feeding or else it will die. Creepy? Sure, a little. But that's what makes it so interesting.

The most convenient way to purchase baking yeast is as a dry, granular product. This is called active dry yeast. *Active* because it's still alive—only *dehydrated*. Add warm liquid and the yeast begins to grow, exhaling carbon dioxide, which creates the little bubbles you see in a loaf of bread.

The type of yeast recommended for the recipes in this book is "quick-rise instant yeast." This product is an extra-speedy breed of yeast, which can be mixed directly into the dry ingredients in the recipe, and will cut the rising time of a yeast dough approximately by half. Purists may frown at this high-speed super-yeast but, frankly, it's nobody's business.

You can also use regular, slow-speed active dry yeast in any of the recipes in this book that call for yeast. (See page 40 for details on how to adjust your recipes.)

Both kinds of active dry yeast are available in individual pre-measured packets or loose in small cans or jars. The loose stuff is more economical if you do a lot of baking. But if you use it only once in a blue moon, the packets are more convenient.

Multigrain Bread

Finishing touches

Just before placing your loaves in the oven, brush the tops with a little beaten egg or milk, sprinkle with a few flakes of rolled oats, and make 3 diagonal slashes across the top of each loaf with a very sharp knife (for that oh-so-trendy professionally slashed look).

Cheerfully wholesome, this bread is delicious toasted for breakfast.

1 cup	250 mL	water
1 cup	250 mL	plain yogurt
¼ cup	50 mL	vegetable oil
½ cup	125 mL	quick-cooking rolled oats (not instant)
⅓ cup	75 mL	wheat germ
⅓ cup	75 mL	unprocessed bran (not bran cereal)
5 ½ cups	1375 mL	all-purpose flour *(approximately)*, divided
¼ cup	50 mL	light brown sugar
4 ½ tsp	22 mL	(2 envelopes) quick-rise instant yeast
2 tsp	10 mL	salt
1		egg

Mix together the water, yogurt and vegetable oil and heat—in the microwave or in a saucepan on the stove—until hot but not boiling. Stir in the oats, wheat germ and bran. Set aside while you organize the rest of the ingredients for the recipe (or run out and buy the stuff you forgot).

In a large bowl, combine 1 cup (250 mL) of the flour, the brown sugar, yeast and salt. Add the warm yogurt mixture and the egg and stir. Using a wooden spoon, continue to stir, adding the remaining flour, ½ cup (125 mL) at a time, until it forms a soft dough. Turn out onto a floured surface and knead by hand (see page 46), sprinkling with more flour just until it is smooth and elastic, and no longer sticky. *(You might not have to use all the flour.)* This should take about 6 to 8 minutes.

Place the dough in an oiled bowl, and turn it over so all the sides of the dough are oiled. Cover with a damp towel or plastic wrap and let rise in a warm place until doubled in size—about 30 to 40 minutes (see page 40).

When the dough has doubled in size, punch it down to deflate it, knead a few times and let it rest while you find the baking pans and grease them. Now form the dough into two loaves (see page 47) and let rise again, until almost twice the size—about 30 minutes.

Preheat the oven to 375° F (190° C).

Bake loaves for 25 to 30 minutes, or until they are nicely browned on top and sound hollow when you tap them. Remove from pans and let cool on a rack before devouring (if you can wait that long).

Variations

Whole Wheat Multigrain Bread

Substitute 1 to 2 cups (250 to 500 mL) whole wheat flour for the same quantity of all-purpose flour in the recipe. The more whole wheat flour you use, the denser the bread will be—so experiment until you know what you like best.

Oatmeal Raisin Multigrain Bread

Omit the wheat germ and bran, and increase the oats to 1 ⅔ cups (400 mL). Soak ½ cup (125 mL) raisins in boiling water for 10 minutes, then drain and stir into the dough along with the egg.

Slow Yeast

Many bakers swear by the traditional kind of active dry yeast, rather than the new quick-rise type. Nothing wrong with that, if you have the time and patience. In fact, you can use it in any recipe that calls for quick-rise yeast—you'll just have to handle it a little differently. It must be diluted with water and activated before use. Like so:

Remove ½ cup (125 mL) of the liquid (water or milk) from the recipe to a small bowl, and heat it until it is just warm to the touch. Stir in 1 tsp (5 mL) of the sugar from the recipe, then sprinkle in the dry yeast granules. Let stand for 5 to 10 minutes. The yeast should begin to bubble and foam in a terribly interesting way. Stir, then add to the dry ingredients along with the remaining liquid. Proceed with the recipe as usual. If the yeast doesn't become foamy, it's probably dead. Start over with fresh stuff.

The rising time will be as much as twice as long as for quick-rise yeast.

Kneading Dough

OK, you've mixed the dough—so far, so good. Now you have to knead it. Right. Like, what's that supposed to mean? Relax—it's fun.

First, a little background. When you look closely at a slice of bread, you'll notice that it's basically a bunch of bubbles in a fibrous framework. This fiber is called gluten—a stretchy protein that occurs in many grains, including wheat (from which most bread dough is made). Without gluten, the little bubbles that give bread its soft and spongy texture would have nothing to hold them together. The bread would collapse and become dense and heavy (like the doorstop your friend Gladys, the health food freak, made for your last potluck party). That is probably not what you had in mind.

But gluten doesn't just *happen*. You have to develop it. That's where kneading comes in. When you work dough by hand (or by machine) you encourage the strands of gluten to become long and elastic so that they can contain the bubbles of carbon dioxide that the yeast exhales as it grows and so that your bread can rise beautifully (see page 40).

The beginner's method

Dust your work surface liberally with flour. Dump the dough out onto this floured surface and dust the top of the dough with more flour. Press down on the dough with the palms of your hands, flattening it to about 1 inch (2 cm) in thickness. Fold it into quarters. Flatten again. Fold again. Continue to flatten and fold, dusting the dough with as much flour as is necessary to keep it from sticking to the table or your hands. Keep going. Don't stop. Flatten, fold, flatten, fold, dust, etc. Eventually the dough will become smooth and elastic and will no longer stick to the table or your hands. Keep kneading a little longer. When it feels *exactly* like your earlobe (pinch it to find out), it's ready. There. Now wasn't that fun?

Advanced transcendental kneading

Eventually you'll become so good at this that you'll no longer have to consciously flatten the dough and fold it into quarters. You can use the heel of one hand to press down on the dough, while simultaneously turning it over with the other. It becomes rhythmic. Hypnotic. Transcendental, man. You become one with the dough as the squishy lump absorbs all your frustration and stress. You achieve inner peace. And, at the same time, you have made bread. I mean, is that perfect or what?

Loafing Around

When it comes to forming a loaf of bread, you have choices, you know. You can, of course, simply form your dough into a regular loaf—the good old kind, squarish, baked in a loaf pan, convenient for sandwiches. Or you could make a fancy braided loaf. Or a round one. Or do something weird and free-form. Go ahead—loaf around.

Regular Loaf

With a rolling pin, roll the dough out on a lightly floured surface, into a 9-inch (23 cm) square (approximately). Now, roll the dough up very firmly into a cylinder, pressing out any air pockets or bubbles. Place it into a well-greased 9 x 5-inch (23 x 13 cm) loaf pan, tucking the ends under neatly. There. Nice and tidy.

Rustic Round Loaf

By hand, form the dough into a firm ball and place it on a well-greased baking sheet that has been lightly sprinkled with cornmeal. Cover with plastic wrap and let rise until almost (but not quite) double. Just before baking, remove the plastic wrap and cut a shallow X in the top of the loaf with a very sharp knife (or a razor blade). When the loaf is baked, this cut will expand, giving your loaf a very snazzy, semiprofessional look.

Beautiful Braided Loaf

For a simple braided loaf, divide the dough into 3 equal pieces and roll each one into a snake, about 1 inch (2 cm) thick. Pinch the 3 pieces together at one end, then braid the strands together until you come to the end. Pinch the end together and place the braid on a well-greased baking sheet.

For a double-decker braided loaf, divide the dough into two unequal portions—one noticeably larger than the other. Working with one portion of dough at a time, form each one into a single braid (as above). Place the smaller braid on top of the larger braid. There. Double decker.

Crazy Mixed-up Loaf

Use your imagination. Make a loaf out of balls of dough squashed into a pan, or roll the dough out into a long snake and form it into a spiral, a squiggle, an octopus, a figure eight. Make a turtle, a bunny, an elephant. Shape your dough into an alligator. A dumptruck. A daisy. Have fun. Go crazy. It'll all get eaten in the end.

Roll 'Em

A dinner roll is nothing more than a teensy loaf of bread. Use any bread dough recipe and make a batch of dinner rolls instead of the usual loaf. They'll bake in about half the time (or less) of a full-sized loaf.

Plain Round Rolls

Form dough into balls, 2 inches (5 cm) across. Place on a well-greased baking sheet, or into the cups of a well-greased muffin pan.

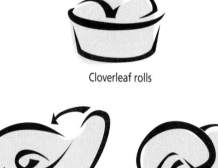

Plain round rolls

Cloverleaf Rolls

Pinch off 1-inch (2 cm) balls of dough, and place 3 of them into each cup of a well-greased muffin pan.

Cloverleaf rolls

Knots

Roll pieces of dough into snakes—about ½ inch (1 cm) thick, and 6 inches (15 cm) long. Tie into a loose knot and place on a well-greased baking sheet, with one end sticking out of the top, and the other one tucked underneath.

Step 1   Step 2

Crescents

With a rolling pin on a lightly floured surface, roll the dough out into a circle, about 12 inches (30 cm) in diameter. Brush the entire surface lightly with melted butter. Cut into 8 to 12 wedges—pizza-wise. Working with one wedge at a time, starting from the outside edge, roll the dough inward toward the point, then place on a well-greased baking sheet and bend lightly to form a crescent. Ta da!

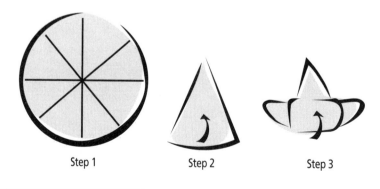

Step 1   Step 2   Step 3

Awesome Egg Challah

This traditional bread is so stunning that it would still be worth making, even if it didn't taste so wonderful.

4 cups	1 liter	all-purpose flour *(approximately)*, divided
4 ½ tsp	22 mL	(2 envelopes) quick-rise instant yeast
¼ cup	50 mL	granulated sugar
2 tsp	10 mL	salt
1 cup	250 mL	hot water
½ cup	125 mL	vegetable oil
3		eggs, lightly beaten
		poppy seeds (optional)

In a very large bowl, stir together 2 cups (500 mL) of the flour, the yeast, sugar and salt. Then add the hot water, oil and two (just two!) of the eggs, and beat with a wooden spoon until smooth. Gradually add the additional flour, ½ cup (125 mL) at a time, until the dough becomes too stiff to stir. It will still be gooey. Dump the dough out onto a well-floured surface and knead until smooth, elastic and feels damp but no longer sticky. (See page 46.) (*You might not have to use all the flour.*)

Grease a large bowl and place the dough into it, turning it over to grease all sides. Cover bowl with plastic wrap and put into a warm place to rise until doubled in size—about 30 to 45 minutes.

Once the dough has risen, punch it down and knead it briefly. Form into one large braided loaf (see page 47) and place on a well-greased baking sheet. Cover with plastic wrap and put back in a warm spot to rise until nearly double—20 to 30 minutes.

Preheat oven to 375° F (190° C).

Beat the remaining egg (remember it?) with 1 tbsp (15 mL) of water. Brush the loaf with this glaze mixture using a pastry brush, sprinkle with some poppy seeds (a lovely but not essential touch) and bake for 30 to 35 minutes, or until the bread is dark golden brown and sounds hollow when you tap it with a finger.

Makes one awesome challah.

Italian Everything Dough

This dough can be used to make the best focaccia you have ever tasted or as a base for your own homemade pizza or both.

Need pizza?

Start with a batch of the basic pizza or focaccia dough. Then keep going:

Preheat the oven to 425° F (220° C).

Cut the dough in half. Roll each half out into a 12-inch (30 cm) circle and place on an oiled pizza pan that has been lightly sprinkled with cornmeal. Pinch the edges up slightly. Spread the dough evenly with spaghetti sauce, cheese, pepperoni, mushrooms, yada, yada, yada. Bake for 20 to 25 minutes, until the crust is browned underneath and the cheese is melted.

Makes two 12-inch (30 cm) pizzas.

3 ½ cups	800 mL	all-purpose flour *(approximately)*, divided
2 ¼ tsp	11 mL	(1 envelope) quick-rise instant yeast
1 tsp	5 mL	salt
1 cup	250 mL	hot water
¼ cup	50 mL	olive or vegetable oil

In a large bowl, stir together 2 cups (500 mL) of the flour, the yeast and salt. Add the hot water and oil and stir until the mixture is smooth (it will be sticky and gooey—don't worry). Now add the remaining flour, ½ cup (125 mL) at a time, stirring it with a wooden spoon until it becomes too sticky to stir.

At this point, dump about ½ cup (125 mL) of the flour onto your counter or table, spread it around a bit, then turn the sticky lump of dough out onto this floured surface. Begin kneading the dough by hand (see page 46), adding only as much additional flour as is necessary to keep it from sticking to your hands (or the table). Continue to knead, for 8 to 10 minutes, until the dough is smooth and elastic. *(You might not have to use all the flour.)*

Place the dough in an oiled bowl. Turn it over to make sure all the sides of the dough are oiled, then cover with plastic wrap and place in a warm spot to rise until double in volume (see page 40)—about 30 minutes.

When the dough has doubled, punch it down to deflate it, then knead it a few more times. Let rest for 5 minutes, and use as a base for pizza or make some phenomenal focaccia (see page 51).

Makes enough dough for two 8 or 9-inch (20 or 23 cm) pans of focaccia, or two 12-inch (30 cm) pizzas.

Phenomenal Phocaccia, er, I Mean Focaccia

After punching down the dough following its first rise, cut the dough in half and roll each half out to fit into a greased 8 or 9-inch (20 or 23 cm) round cake pan.

Top with whatever weird and wonderful toppings you like (inspirations below), cover loosely with plastic wrap and let rise again until almost double—about 20 to 30 minutes.

Preheat the oven to 375° F (190° C).

Place baking pans on the lowest rack of the oven and bake for 25 to 30 minutes, until the dough is lightly browned on the edges and the center of the focaccia is no longer gooey (stick a fork into it to check).

Just *try* to resist eating the whole thing immediately.

Makes two 8 or 9-inch (20 or 23 cm) pans of focaccia.

Focaccia Inspirations

Each of the following combinations is enough to top one 8 or 9-inch (20 or 23 cm) round focaccia. Feel free to completely ignore these suggestions.

Mainly Mediterranean

¼ cup	50 mL	chopped brine-cured olives
¼ cup	50 mL	chopped sun-dried tomatoes
½ cup	125 mL	crumbled feta cheese
		salt, pepper and crumbled rosemary

Somewhat Sicilian

1		onion, sliced and sauteed in olive oil
1		small ripe tomato, very thinly sliced
¼ cup	50 mL	grated Parmesan cheese
		salt, pepper and crumbled oregano

Perfectly Pesto

¼ cup	50 mL	pesto
¼ cup	50 mL	chopped sun-dried tomatoes
½ cup	125 mL	crumbled goat cheese

Not Quite Naked

2 tbsp	30 mL	olive oil
2		cloves garlic, chopped
		salt, pepper and crumbled rosemary

The Clueless Baker

Universal Sweet Dough

One batch of this dough can be used to make a multitude of delights. You can even use half of the dough to bake a pan of cinnamon buns (see page 54), and the other half to make a bubble bread (see page 56). Perfect if you just can't decide what you want.

4 ½ cups	1 liter	all-purpose flour *(approximately)*, divided
⅓ cup	75 mL	granulated sugar
4 ½ tsp	22 mL	(2 envelopes) quick-rise instant yeast
1 tsp	5 mL	salt
¾ cup	175 mL	milk
½ cup	125 mL	water
⅓ cup	75 mL	butter
2		eggs

In a large bowl, stir together 2 cups (500 mL) of the flour (pay attention—this is only *part* of the flour) with the sugar, yeast and salt.

In a small saucepan or heatproof measuring cup, combine the milk, water and butter. Heat until it is just uncomfortably warm to the touch, then add to the flour mixture. Beat with an electric mixer (or by hand with a wooden spoon) until it forms a stringy, sticky, gloppy batter. Add the eggs and then add the remaining flour ½ cup (125 mL) at a time, beating or stirring well until it becomes too difficult to stir. Now dump the dough out onto a well-floured surface and knead by hand for 6 to 8 minutes, sprinkling with additional flour to keep it from sticking to your hands or the table. *(You might not have to use all the flour.)* When the dough is no longer sticky, and feels like a damp earlobe when you pinch it, it's ready. Place it in an oiled bowl, turning it over to oil the top. Cover with plastic wrap and let rise until double—about 30 to 40 minutes.

Punch the dough to deflate it. Knead it a few times, then shape. Now you're ready to bake it in any of the following incredibly easy, but terribly impressive, ways.

Cinnamon Rolls

Use half of one batch of the Universal Sweet Dough to make one pan of these cinnamon buns. Do something else with the rest of the dough, or repeat and make another pan to freeze for a rainy day.

½ recipe		Universal Sweet Dough (see page 53)
½ cup	125 mL	light brown sugar
1 tsp	5 mL	cinnamon
¼ cup	50 mL	softened butter
⅓ cup	75 mL	raisins or dried cranberries

Prepare the Universal Sweet Dough and divide in half. Use one half for this recipe and reserve the rest for another recipe.

In a small bowl, combine the brown sugar with the cinnamon.

With a rolling pin, roll the dough out on a lightly floured surface to form a rectangle approximately 9 x 12 inches (23 x 30 cm) in size. Spread as evenly as possible with the softened butter. Sprinkle with the cinnamon-sugar mixture and the raisins or cranberries. Starting with a short end, roll dough up as tightly as possible—pinch the loose end to keep it from unravelling. Cut into 9 slices and arrange, spiral side up, in a well-greased 8 or 9-inch (20 or 23 cm) square baking pan. Cover with plastic wrap and let rise until nearly double (about 30 minutes).

Preheat the oven to 375° F (190° C)

Bake for 25 to 30 minutes, or until buns are nicely browned on top and sound hollow when you tap them with your finger. Drizzle with Shiny Sugar Glaze (see page 167) and let cool slightly before devouring.

Makes 9 buns.

Sticky Bun Variation

Prepare the Cinnamon Bun recipe (see page 56). But before you put the buns into the baking pan, do the following:

In a small saucepan, combine ½ cup (125 mL) each butter, light brown sugar and chopped pecans or walnuts. Heat just until the butter is melted and stir until the mixture is mixed. Spread in the bottom of a 8 or 9-inch (20 or 23 cm) square baking pan. Top with the unbaked cinnamon buns (remember them?).

Cover, let rise, bake, bla bla bla—just the same as for normal cinnamon buns. Only better. Turn upside down to remove from the pan.

Chocolate Rolls

Instead of using cinnamon-sugar as a filling, spread the rolled-out dough with a thick layer of chocolate fudge sauce (store-bought ice cream stuff from a jar is fine) before rolling and cutting into slices. Prepare as for the cinnamon buns. After baking, cool buns and then drizzle them with Chocolate Ganache Glaze (see page 166).

Bubble Bread

Make Cinnamon Rolls (see page 54) with half of the batch of Universal Sweet Dough and make this with the other half. Very fun.

½ recipe		Universal Sweet Dough (see page 53)
¾ cup	175 mL	granulated sugar
1 ½ tsp	7 mL	cinnamon
½ cup	125 mL	melted butter
½ cup	125 mL	raisins
½ cup	125 mL	chopped walnuts or pecans

Prepare the Universal Sweet Dough and divide in half. Use one half for this recipe and reserve the rest for another recipe.

In a small bowl, stir together the cinnamon and sugar. Pour the melted butter into another small bowl.

Grease a 9-inch (23 cm) bundt pan.

Now—here's what you do. Pinch off pieces of dough, about 1 inch (2 cm) across and roll into small balls. One at a time, dunk each ball first in the melted butter, then roll in the cinnamon-sugar. Arrange in the bundt pan. When you have a layer of dough balls, sprinkle on some of the raisins and nuts. Continue adding balls and sprinkling nuts and raisins, until all the dough is used up and arranged evenly in the baking pan. Cover and let rise until almost double—about 30 minutes.

Preheat the oven to 375° F (190° C).

Bake for 30 to 35 minutes, until golden brown. Invert pan and remove Bubble Bread to a rack to cool. A drizzle of Shiny Sugar Glaze (see page 167) is a nice (but optional) finishing touch.

Makes one very nifty Bubble Bread.

Clueless Troubleshooting: Quick Breads and Yeast Breads

OK, so your bread didn't turn out so good. It's dense as a doorstop and tastes like, well, you don't actually know because you can't chew it. It's OK—we've all been there. The following problems have all been experienced by ordinary persons (such as yourself), many of whom have gone on to live perfectly normal lives. And, yes, bake bread again.

Quick Breads

It didn't rise at all.
- Did you remember to add the baking powder or baking soda? It's pretty important.
- How old is your baking powder or baking soda? Has it been in your cupboard for five years? Is it the same stuff you use to deodorize the refrigerator? Treat yourself to a fresh box—you deserve it.
- Did you let the batter sit around for a long time? Baking soda and baking powder begin working as soon as the batter is mixed. With time, the batter may lose its get-up-and-go. Get up and get it into the oven more quickly next time.

It rose nicely, then collapsed.
- Was it fully baked when you took it out of the oven? Are you sure? Do the toothpick test next time (see page 28).
- Don't open the oven door any more than you absolutely have to. A cold draft can make a quick bread cranky and cause it to collapse.

Ack—my bread is lopsided!
- Your oven may not heat evenly, causing some areas to be hotter than others. Turning the bread pans around midway through the baking time may help avoid lopsidedness. Move them back to front and switch oven racks. This may not totally cure the problem but could reduce it.

- Are your oven racks bent? Check them. If the baking pan is on a slant, your bread will be too.

The bottom burned before the bread was done.

- If your oven heats unevenly, you can try moving your bread pans to a higher shelf next time. Or simply lower the heat by 10 to 25 degrees.
- Get an oven thermometer and use it to check if your oven is behaving itself.

The batter overflowed the pan!

- Your pan may have been too small for the amount of batter. Check the volume of the baking pan or measure the diameter to make sure you're using the correct pan for the recipe.
- Or maybe you added too much baking powder or baking soda.

My bread is stuck in the pan.

- Grease the pan with non-stick cooking spray next time.
- Or line the bottom with parchment.
- Or both.

The breads look fine, but they have a weird taste.

- If your dry ingredients weren't thoroughly mixed, you may have lumps of baking soda or baking powder that can give baked goods a creepy flavor. Be sure to mix (or even sift) the dry ingredients together before adding the liquids.
- Have your ingredients gone rancid? Nothing can disguise the taste of old nuts, oil or whole wheat flour. Their flavor will permeate everything and make even the most wonderful loaf of bread taste icky. Buy fresh ingredients and store them in the refrigerator or freezer.

Yeast Breads

The yeast bread didn't rise at all.

- Dead yeast. Maybe it died of old age (has it been in your cupboard for five years?), in which case you'll have to buy a fresh package. Or maybe you killed it (you fiend!) by adding liquid that was too hot. Try again and be more careful next time.
- Cold dough. Was your rising spot too cool? Try warming it up by placing the bowl in a larger bowl filled with warm (not hot) water and giving it more time.

The dough didn't rise enough.

- Low-gluten-content flour—like cake and pastry flour—won't develop the stretchy framework that allows a yeast bread to hold its shape. It's like trying to construct an apartment building out of applesauce. Use all-purpose flour or (if you are serious about this) bread flour.
- Dough was just too heavy. Too many whole grains or other additions (raisins, seeds, cracked wheat, oats, etc.) will keep a bread dough from rising sufficiently. Poor thing just can't lift itself up. Cut back on the "stuff" or just learn to enjoy dense bread.

It rose, then collapsed.

- Your rising spot was too warm. Find a slightly cooler spot next time.
- You let the dough rise too long. If you can't bake your bread as soon as it has doubled in size, punch it down and put it in a cool place (like the refrigerator) to buy yourself some more time. If you allow the dough to over-rise, it simply can't support itself anymore and will collapse.

The bread browned too quickly.

- Your oven is too hot. Don't feel bad, it happens to the nicest ovens. Have you checked the temperature with an oven thermometer? Even 10 degrees can make a noticeable difference.
- Too much sugar (or honey or other sweetener) in your dough. Reduce the amount of sweetener next time.
- Did you glaze the top of the bread with egg yolk? It can cause the bread to over-brown. Omit the glaze next time—or learn to appreciate the effect.

The loaf didn't brown enough.

- The oven isn't hot enough. Check the temperature with an oven thermometer to make sure it's accurate.
- Use an egg yolk glaze next time. It will give you a darker crust.

My bread looks like Swiss cheese.

- Your dough rose too quickly. Maybe your rising spot is too warm. Find another place.
- The dough wasn't punched down enough, leaving big air pockets in it. Next time you make bread, knead it for a couple of minutes after punching it down, to eliminate big bubbles.

My free-form loaves look like giant pancakes!

- Your shaped dough was allowed to rise too long before baking. It got tired and could no longer hold itself up in a nice loaf shape. Next time, put the bread in the oven *before* the shaped loaves have fully doubled in size. They will continue to rise when they go into the oven.
- The dough was too soft. If you're planning to bake a free-form loaf, make a slightly stiffer dough by kneading in a little extra flour. It will hold its shape better and not spread out as much.

The top of the bread has split.

- Hey, it happens. Next time, avoid unsightly splits by taking a very sharp knife (or utility blade) and making a few slashes in the top of the unbaked loaf just before it goes into the oven. You'll still have splits, but at least they'll be pretty ones.

The bread was overdone on top, but underdone on the bottom (or vice versa).

- Check your oven temperature with an oven thermometer. If it's too hot, the outsides will look done before the insides are properly baked. Adjust the temperature to compensate for this.
- The heat in your oven may be uneven. Place loaves on a lower shelf if the top is cooking too quickly, or on a higher shelf if the bottom is burning.

Muffins and Biscuits

They go with coffee. They go with soup. They can go it alone. Butter them or don't. Spread them with cream cheese or strawberry jam. Eat them plain. In a car. On a bus. At the breakfast table. A batch of freshly baked muffins or biscuits can turn a panful of carelessly scrambled eggs into a perfectly respectable brunch, or a bowl of leftover chili into a two-course dinner.

Muffins

Beautiful Buttermilk Muffins

Start with a basic buttermilk muffin—and have your way with it. Add blueberries or poppy seeds or (gasp) chocolate chips. Add stuff we haven't even thought of. Muffins are so personal, don't you think?

1 cup	250 mL	buttermilk or sour milk (see page 17)
¾ cup	175 mL	granulated sugar
½ cup	125 mL	vegetable oil
2		eggs
1 tsp	5 mL	vanilla zest
1 tsp	5 mL	grated lemon peel
2 cups	500 mL	all-purpose flour
2 tsp	10 mL	baking powder
½ tsp	2 mL	baking soda

Preheat the oven to 375° F (190° C). Grease a 12-cup muffin pan.

In a large bowl, beat together the sugar, oil, eggs, vanilla and lemon zest until light(ish).

In another bowl, mix together the flour, baking powder and baking soda. Stir this mixture into the egg mixture, in 2 or 3 additions, alternating with the buttermilk. Beat only until combined—don't overbeat!—then spoon the batter into the well-greased (or paper-lined) muffin pan, filling the cups nearly to the top. Bake for 20 to 25 minutes, until lightly browned on top.

Makes 12 muffins.

Variations

Blueberry Muffins

Stir 1 cup (250 mL) fresh or frozen (don't defrost them!) blueberries into the batter before spooning it into the muffin pan. Bake as for Beautiful Buttermilk Muffins.

Chocolate Chip Muffins

Stir 1 cup (250 mL) chocolate chips into the batter before spooning it into the muffin pan. Bake as for Beautiful Buttermilk Muffins.

Poppy Seed Muffins

Mix ¼ cup (50 mL) poppy seeds into the buttermilk and let soak while you prepare the rest of the ingredients. Add to the batter and bake as for Beautiful Buttermilk Muffins.

Cranberry or Cherry Muffins

Stir 1 cup (250 mL) of chopped dried cranberries or dried cherries into the batter before baking. Bake as for Beautiful Buttermilk Muffins.

Honey Bran Muffins

Measuring honey or molasses

Measuring honey, molasses or any other sticky liquid is a yucky, messy business. But not if you plan ahead. Before you pour the honey into the measuring cup, first use it to measure any oil or melted shortening you're using in the recipe. The honey will then slide right out of the oil-coated measuring cup. If there's no oil in your recipe, just spray the inside of the cup with non-stick baking spray instead.

These excellent muffins will make you feel virtuous and healthy. This is a good thing at breakfast time, because we all know it goes downhill from there.

½ cup	125 mL	vegetable oil
½ cup	125 mL	honey
1		egg
1 cup	250 mL	all-purpose flour
1 tsp	5 mL	baking soda
1 cup	250 mL	buttermilk, plain yogurt or sour milk (see page 17)
1 ½ cups	375 mL	natural bran (not bran cereal)
½ cup	125 mL	raisins (optional)

Preheat the oven to 375° F (190° C). Grease a 12-cup muffin pan.

In a large bowl, whisk together the vegetable oil, honey and egg until smooth. In a small bowl, combine the flour with the baking soda. Add the flour mixture to the egg mixture in 2 or 3 portions, alternating with the buttermilk (or yogurt, or sour milk), stirring just until everything is evenly moistened. Stir in the bran and the raisins if you're using them.

Spoon batter into the well-greased (or paper-lined) muffin pan, filling the cups almost to the top. Bake for 20 to 25 minutes, until a toothpick poked into the middle of a muffin comes out clean.

Makes 10 to 12 muffins.

Blender Peanut Butter Muffins

Plain, chocolate chip, or filled with jelly. A glass of cold milk is mandatory.

2 cups	500 mL	all-purpose flour
¼ cup	50 mL	granulated sugar
1 tsp	5 mL	baking powder
½ tsp	2 mL	baking soda
1 cup	250 mL	creamy peanut butter
1 cup	250 mL	milk
2		eggs
1 tsp	5 mL	vanilla
1 cup	250 mL	semisweet chocolate chips (optional!)

Preheat the oven to 400° F (200° C). Grease a 12-cup muffin pan.

In a large bowl, stir together the flour, sugar, baking powder and baking soda.

In the container of a blender or food processor, combine the peanut butter, milk, eggs and vanilla. Blend or process until smooth. Add to the flour mixture, stirring just until everything is evenly moistened and combined.

Now mix in the chocolate chips, if you're using them, then spoon the batter into the well-greased (or paper-lined) muffin pan, filling the cups to the top. Bake for 15 to 20 minutes, until the muffins are lightly browned and a toothpick poked into the middle of a muffin comes out clean.

Makes about 12 muffins.

What about peanut butter and jelly?

The classic combo in a muffin. Here's what you do. Leave the batter plain (no chocolate chips) and fill each muffin cup half full. Place 1 tsp (5 mL) of your favorite jam or jelly in the middle of each muffin, then cover completely with the remaining batter. Bake as usual. Yum.

And if that isn't scrumptious enough...

Top each unbaked muffin with a sprinkle of All-Purpose Crumble Topping (see page 176). Bake as if it were perfectly normal. Which, of course, it isn't.

Oatmeal Raisin Muffins (or Not)

Plump those raisins!

Instead of just tossing a bunch of raisins into the batter—why don't you plump them first? Don't be shy—it's not embarrassing. Here's what you do:

Measure your raisins into a bowl and cover them with boiling water. Or pour water over the raisins and microwave them for 2 minutes. Let them sit while you prepare the rest of the recipe, then drain them and add them to whatever you're making. The raisins will come out soft and, well, plump, in whatever you're making. This is especially useful in recipes where the baking time is short (like muffins), and the raisins wouldn't otherwise have time to soften in the oven.

Purists may prefer to omit the raisins. That's fine. Or you could substitute chocolate chips for the raisins, if you're feeling reckless.

1 cup	250 mL	quick-cooking rolled oats (not instant)
1 cup	250 mL	buttermilk, plain yogurt or sour milk (see page 17)
1		egg
⅓ cup	75 mL	light brown sugar
¼ cup	50 mL	vegetable oil
1 cup	250 mL	all-purpose flour
1 tsp	5 mL	baking powder
½ tsp	2 mL	baking soda
½ cup	125 mL	raisins (or chocolate chips, or nothing)

Preheat the oven to 400° F (200° C). Grease a 12-cup muffin pan.

In a bowl, stir together the rolled oats and the buttermilk (or whatever you're using). Let soak for 10 minutes or so, then stir in the egg, brown sugar, and vegetable oil.

In another bowl, stir together the flour, baking powder and baking soda. Add this mixture to the oat mixture and stir just until combined. Add the raisins (or whatever) if you're using them. Spoon batter into the well-greased (or paper-lined) muffin pan, filling the cups almost to the top. Bake for 18 to 20 minutes, or until the tops spring back when you touch them and are lightly browned. Let cool slightly before serving (but they're really best while they're still warm).

Makes 9 to 10 muffins.

Cranberry Cornmeal Muffins

You can leave out the dried cranberries if you prefer a basic cornmeal muffin—to serve with a bowl of chili, for instance.

1 ½ cups	375 mL	all-purpose flour
1 cup	250 mL	yellow cornmeal
¼ cup	50 mL	granulated sugar
2 tbsp	30 mL	baking powder
½ tsp	2 mL	salt
¼ cup	50 mL	vegetable oil
1		egg
1 ⅓ cups	325 mL	milk
½ cup	125 mL	dried cranberries, chopped (optional)

Preheat the oven to 400° F (200° C). Grease a 12-cup muffin pan.

In a large bowl, stir together the flour, cornmeal, sugar, baking powder and salt. In a smaller bowl, beat together the oil, egg and milk. Now pour the milk mixture into the flour mixture and stir together with a wooden spoon until pretty well combined. A few lumps are no big deal so don't overbeat it. Stir in the chopped cranberries, if you're using them.

Spoon the batter into the well-greased (or paper-lined) muffin pan, filling the cups to the top. Bake for about 15 minutes, or until very lightly browned and the tops spring back when you touch them. Remove from pan and serve warm.

Makes 12 large muffins, which really do lose some of their charm once they're cool.

Don't leave your muffin cups empty

When there's not enough batter to fill all the cups in a muffin pan, fill the empty ones with water. It will add a little humidity to the oven (a good thing) and prevent the pan from scorching.

Triple-Grain Apple Muffins

There's always room for improvement

Sprinkle the top of each unbaked muffin with a bit of All-Purpose Crumble Topping (see page 176), which you have cleverly stashed in a container in the freezer for just such an occasion. Bake the muffins as if they were naked.

These are hearty and nutritious—but in a good way. A perfect muffin to start your day.

¾ cup	175 mL	all-purpose flour
½ cup	125 mL	quick-cooking rolled oats
½ cup	125 mL	bran
¼ cup	50 mL	cornmeal
½ cup	125 mL	light brown sugar
1 tbsp	15 mL	baking powder
¼ tsp	1 mL	cinnamon
1		egg
½ cup	125 mL	milk
¼ cup	50 mL	vegetable oil
1 cup	250 mL	coarsely grated apple (approximately 1 large or 2 small apples, peeled and cored)

Preheat the oven to 400° F (200° C). Grease a 12-cup muffin pan.

In a large mixing bowl, stir together the flour, oats, bran, cornmeal, light brown sugar, baking powder and cinnamon.

In another bowl, beat the egg with the milk and the vegetable oil. Add the egg mixture to the flour mixture and stir until all the ingredients are evenly moistened (don't overbeat—muffins *hate* it when that happens!). Mix in the grated apple, stirring just until combined.

Spoon the batter into a well-greased (or paper-lined) muffin pan, filling the cups to the top. Bake for 18 to 20 minutes, until the muffins are lightly browned and a toothpick poked into the middle of one comes out clean. Remove from pan and place on a rack to cool. Or just eat them right away.

Makes 8 to 10 muffins.

Coleslaw Muffins

Don't panic. They only look like coleslaw—they don't taste like it.

2 cups	500 mL	shredded apples (peeled or unpeeled)
1 cup	250 mL	shredded carrot
1 cup	250 mL	granulated sugar
1 cup	250 mL	dried cranberries or raisins, coarsely chopped
1 cup	250 mL	chopped walnuts
2 ½ cups	625 mL	all-purpose flour
1 tbsp	15 mL	baking powder
2 tsp	10 mL	baking soda
1 tsp	5 mL	cinnamon
2		eggs
½ cup	125 mL	vegetable oil

Preheat the oven to 375° F (190° F). Grease a 12-cup muffin pan.

In a large bowl, combine the shredded apples, shredded carrot and sugar, tossing to mix. Stir in the dried cranberries or raisins and walnuts.

In another bowl, stir together the flour, baking powder, baking soda and cinnamon. Dump into the apple mixture and stir to blend.

Beat together the eggs and oil and add this to the batter, stirring until everything is evenly combined. Spoon batter into the well-greased (or paper-lined) muffin pan, filling the cups almost to the top. Bake for 25 to 30 minutes, until golden brown.

Makes about 12 muffins.

Cappuccino Chip Muffins

You're sitting at a cafe, reading something obscure, written by a nine-teenth-century French philosopher that no one has heard of. You're drinking an espresso. And eating a muffin. You don't need to explain anything.

2 cups	500 mL	all-purpose flour
½ cup	125 mL	granulated sugar
1 tbsp	15 mL	baking powder
1 tbsp	15 mL	instant coffee powder
½ tsp	2 mL	cinnamon
1 cup	250 mL	milk
1		egg
½ cup	125 mL	vegetable oil
½ cup	125 mL	semisweet chocolate chips

Preheat the oven to 375° F (190° C). Grease a 12-cup muffin pan.

In a large bowl, stir together the flour, sugar, baking powder, instant coffee and cinnamon. (If your instant coffee is in big chunky crystals, crush it into a powder before adding so that it mixes more easily.)

In another bowl, beat together the milk, egg and vegetable oil. Add to the flour mixture and stir until just combined. Mix in the chocolate chips. Don't overbeat—just mix everything together and leave it alone.

Spoon batter into the well-greased (or paper-lined) muffin pan, filling the cups to the top. Bake for 18 to 20 minutes, or until they pass the toothpick test (see page 28). Remove from the pan and let cool slightly before serving. If you can stand to wait that long.

Makes about 8 muffins.

Chocolate Chocolate Muffins

OK, here's where we draw the line. These muffins are absolutely not a healthy breakfast item. They are not low fat, or low cholesterol, or low anything. For your own good, we recommend that you not eat the whole batch at once.

2 cups	500 mL	all-purpose flour
1 cup	250 mL	granulated sugar
1 tsp	5 mL	baking soda
½ cup	125 mL	butter
3 squares		(1 oz/28 g each) unsweetened chocolate
1 cup	250 mL	buttermilk, yogurt or sour milk (see page 17)
1		egg
2 tsp	10 mL	vanilla
1 cup	250 mL	semisweet chocolate chips

Preheat the oven to 400° F (200° C). Grease a 12-cup muffin pan.

In a medium bowl, stir together the flour, sugar and baking soda. Set it aside.

In a medium saucepan over low heat, melt together the butter and the unsweetened chocolate (broken into chunks to hurry things up). Stir until smooth, then remove from heat and let cool for just a minute. Add the buttermilk, egg and vanilla, whisking the mixture until everything is well combined. Stir in the flour mixture, mixing just until all the ingredients are moistened, then add the chocolate chips. Mix until the chips are evenly distributed. Then stop.

Spoon batter into the well-greased (or paper-lined) muffin pan, filling the cups to the top. Bake for 15 to 20 minutes, or until a toothpick poked into the middle of a muffin comes out clean. Let cool for a couple of minutes before removing from the pan, then transfer to a rack to cool more or less completely.

Yikes. Makes 10 chocolate chocolate muffins.

Variation

Chocolate chocolate chocolate muffins

Drizzle the muffins with Chocolate Ganache Glaze (see page 166) if you want to be *really* bad.

Biscuits

Go-With-Anything Biscuits

Go-with-any-thing butter-milk biscuits

Tangy buttermilk gives biscuits an added dimension. If you happen to have some around, try this: reduce the baking powder to 2 tsp (10 mL) and substitute buttermilk for the regular milk in the basic recipe. Otherwise bake as usual.

These biscuits are just as good with butter and jam for breakfast as they are plunked on top of a stew for supper.

2 cups	500 mL	all-purpose flour
1 tbsp	15 mL	baking powder
1 tsp	5 mL	granulated sugar
½ tsp	2 mL	salt
⅓ cup	75 mL	cold unsalted butter
¾ cup	175 mL	milk

Preheat the oven to 450° F (230° C).

In a mixing bowl, or in a food processor, mix together the flour, baking powder, sugar and salt. Add the butter to the flour mixture, cutting it in with a pastry blender (or by running the processor) until the mixture looks like coarse cornmeal. If you're using a processor, dump the mixture out into a bowl. By hand, stir in the milk and mix until it forms a soft dough. Transfer to a lightly floured surface and knead 10 or 12 times, until it's pliable.

With a rolling pin, roll the dough out until it's about ½ inch (1 cm) thick. Cut with a round cookie cutter (2 inches/5 cm is a good size) and place on an ungreased baking sheet. Bake for 12 to 14 minutes, until lightly browned on top and nicely puffed.

Serve warm. With anything.

Makes about 8 biscuits.

Cheddar Biscuits

These are great with a bowl of soup, but there's no law against serving them with scrambled eggs or split in half with thin slices of ham or salami.

2 cups	500 mL	all-purpose flour
1 tbsp	15 mL	baking powder
1 tbsp	15 mL	granulated sugar
½ tsp	2 mL	salt
¼ cup	50 mL	cold unsalted butter
1 ¼ cups	300 mL	shredded cheddar cheese
¾ cup	175 mL	milk

Choose your cheese

No cheddar in your refrigerator? No problem. Use whatever cheese you happen to have—even a mixture of shrivelled odds and ends—Swiss, Monterey jack, havarti, provolone, even blue cheese. Very interesting.

Preheat the oven to 450° F (230° C).

In a large bowl, or in a food processor, mix together the flour, baking powder, sugar and salt. Cut in the butter with a pastry blender (or by running the processor) until the mixture looks like coarse cornmeal. If you're using a processor, transfer mixture to a bowl. By hand, stir in the shredded cheese and toss to combine. Add the milk all at once and stir until it forms a soft dough. Dump out onto a lightly floured surface and knead by hand 10 or 12 times.

With a rolling pin, roll out the dough to ½-inch (1 cm) thickness. Cut into rounds (2 inches (5 cm) is a good size) and place on an ungreased baking sheet. Bake for 12 to 14 minutes, until the biscuits are lightly browned and nicely puffed.

Makes 8 to 10 biscuits.

Herb and Garlic Olive Oil Scones

Handy herbs

You can use any mixture of dried herbs you like to make these scones. If you don't have a ready-made blend, just mix up a combination of oregano, rosemary, thyme, basil— whatever herbs you like. Or, better yet, if you happen to have fresh herbs, use 2 tbsp (30 mL), finely chopped, instead of the dried mixture.

These make a deadly delicious appetizer with a bit of cheese and a few olives. Or serve them with a bowl of soup. Impossibly easy.

2 cups	500 mL	all-purpose flour
1 tbsp	15 mL	baking powder
¼ cup	50 mL	grated Parmesan cheese
½ tsp	2 mL	salt
¼ tsp	1 mL	black pepper
½ cup	125 mL	plain yogurt
⅓ cup	75 mL	olive oil
1		egg
1		clove garlic, minced
1 tbsp	15 mL	crumbled *herbes de Provence* or Italian spices (see sidebar)

Preheat the oven to 375° F (190° C).

In a large bowl, mix together the flour, baking powder, Parmesan cheese, salt and pepper.

In another bowl, whisk together the yogurt, oil, egg, garlic and crumbled herbs until it forms a gloppy mixture. Add this to the flour mixture, stirring until it forms a soft dough. Dump the dough out onto a lightly floured surface and knead 10 or 12 strokes until it's smooth and pliable. Divide into two lumps.

With a rolling pin, roll out one lump of dough into a 5-inch (13 cm) circle. With a sharp knife, cut it pizza-wise into 8 wedges. Place the wedges on a lightly greased baking sheet. Repeat with the second half of the dough.

Bake for 15 to 20 minutes, until ever so slightly browned on top. Serve immediately (they're not nearly as good cold).

Makes 16 scones.

Fruit Yogurt Scones

Lovely with a pot of Earl Grey tea, creamy butter and strawberry jam.

2 ½ cups	**575 mL**	**all-purpose flour**
1 tbsp	**15 mL**	**baking powder**
¼ cup	**50 mL**	**granulated sugar**
½ cup	**125 mL**	**cold butter, cut into chunks**
¾ cup	**175 mL**	**any type of fruit yogurt**

Preheat the oven to 425° F (220° C).

Measure the flour, baking powder and sugar into a large bowl. Stir to mix well. Add the butter chunks and, using a pastry blender or two knives, cut the butter into the flour mixture until it looks evenly crumbly (see page 173).

Add the yogurt to the crumbly mixture and stir just until it forms a soft dough that will cling together in a ball. Dump the dough out onto a lightly floured surface and knead it by hand about 10 or 12 times *just* until it's smooth. Please resist, if possible, the temptation to overwork the dough. Excessive kneading will make the scones tough.

By hand (or gently, with a rolling pin) pat the dough down on a well-floured surface to about 1-inch (2 cm) thickness. Cut into circles with a 2-inch (5 cm) cookie cutter or cut with a knife into triangles (a more traditional scone shape).

Place scones on an ungreased baking sheet, slightly apart (to allow for rising), and bake for 12 to 15 minutes, until lightly browned.

Makes 12 to 16 terribly dainty scones.

Quick Little Dinner Buns

Not a muffin, but not exactly a regular dinner roll either. These buns are incredibly easy to make and are great with a bowl of homemade soup.

2 cups	500 mL	all-purpose flour
2 tsp	10 mL	baking powder
½ tsp	2 mL	salt
1 ½ cups	375 mL	milk
6 tbsp	90 mL	mayonnaise

Preheat the oven to 400° F (200° C). Grease a 12-cup muffin pan.

In a mixing bowl, stir together the flour, baking powder and salt. Add the milk and mayonnaise, and stir with a fork until everything is blended and the mixture is smooth. Spoon into a well-greased (or paper-lined) muffin pan, filling the cups about ⅔ full. Bake for 20 to 25 minutes, until the tops are lightly browned.

Remove from pan, let cool slightly and serve warm.

Makes 8 to 10 quick little buns.

Clueless Troubleshooting: Muffins and Biscuits

Muffins and biscuits should be simple and straightforward and give you no trouble at all. But sometimes they misbehave. Here's some help in tracking down the problem so that next time you can show them who's boss.

They didn't rise at all.

- Did you add the baking powder or baking soda? Are you sure you added it?
- How old is your baking powder/soda? Older than your car? Buy a fresh package—it doesn't last forever.
- Did the batter hang around too long before baking? While it is sometimes OK to let the batter sit for a while before baking, not all recipes can handle the wait. If your recipe says to put it in the oven right away—*do it.*

They rose nicely, then collapsed.

- Did you take them out of the oven before they were fully baked? Do the toothpick test next time (see page 28).
- Don't open the oven door every two minutes to see how they're doing. Fluctuating oven temperature can cause muffins to collapse.

The bottoms burned before the muffins or biscuits were fully baked.

- Try moving your pan to a higher shelf next time. Or simply lower the heat by 10 to 25 degrees. Your oven may heat unevenly.
- Get an oven thermometer and use it.

My muffins are pointy. What's up with that?

- The batter was overbeaten. Didn't we tell you not to do that?

All the blueberries sank to the bottom of the muffins.

- Toss the blueberries with a little of the flour from the recipe before adding them to the batter to keep them suspended in the muffin.

My muffins refuse to come out of the pan.

- Invest in a non-stick muffin pan.
- Grease the cups with non-stick cooking spray.
- If all else fails, use paper cupcake liners.

The muffins look fine, but they taste, uh, funny.

- The dry ingredients may not have been thoroughly mixed. Lumps of baking soda or baking powder can give baked goods a creepy flavor. Make sure you mix (or even sift) the dry ingredients together before adding the liquids.
- Were your ingredients fresh? Really now—were they? Nothing can disguise the taste of rancid nuts, oil or whole wheat flour. Throw the muffins away. Or feed them to the birds. Treat yourself to fresh ingredients and keep them refrigerated.

Cookies and Squares

You don't need a reason to bake cookies. Cookies exist in a universe all their own—pointless but wonderful. A tiny bit of something delicious, which can be eaten without a fork or plate. Cookies can be stuffed into a brown paper lunch bag, piled in a frayed wicker basket or arranged tastefully on an antique silver platter. It makes no difference—a good cookie is always an excellent thing.

Cookies

Crisp Oatmeal Cookies

This is a classic oatmeal cookie—crisp enough to be improved by dunking into a glass of chocolate milk.

½ cup	125 mL	butter
½ cup	125 mL	granulated sugar
½ cup	125 mL	light brown sugar
1		egg
1 tsp	5 mL	vanilla
1 cup	250 mL	all-purpose or whole wheat flour (or a mixture)
½ tsp	2 mL	baking powder
½ tsp	2 mL	baking soda
½ cup	125 mL	quick-cooking rolled oats (not instant)
1 cup	250 mL	unsweetened shredded coconut

Preheat the oven to 375° F (190° C).

In a large mixing bowl, with an electric mixer, beat together the butter, granulated and brown sugars, egg and vanilla until blended and creamy.

Add the flour, baking powder and baking soda and beat until mixed. Now stir in the oats and coconut—mix well.

Drop dough by teaspoonfuls onto an ungreased cookie sheet, leaving 2 inches (5 cm) between them to allow for spreading. Bake for 9 to 12 minutes, until lightly browned around the edges.

Makes 3 dozen cookies.

Baker's Parchment Paper

Baker's parchment is a heavy, unwaxed paper, specifically intended to be used for cooking and baking. If you don't already have a roll of the stuff in your cupboard, you should run out right now and buy some. It's better than waxed paper for lining the bottom of cake pans (so that your cakes don't stick), and is an absolute miracle for baking cookies. A cookie sheet lined with baking parchment can be reused several times before the paper has to be replaced, and will leave you with a perfectly clean baking sheet after you're all done. The non-stick surface may also allow you to either eliminate greasing the pan altogether, or to just give your pan a very light greasing.

You can also use parchment paper for other cooking purposes—like cooking fish or chicken in fancy little packets or covering a casserole to retain moisture.

In a pinch, it can even be used to trace a map of South America for that geography project your kid has to finish Wednesday.

Big Chewy Oatmeal Raisin Cookies

Help! My brown sugar is hard as a rock!

Don't panic. Just put one quarter of a fresh apple into an airtight container with the hard sugar and go away for 24 hours. When you come back, the apple will look as if it's had a rough night, but your brown sugar will be perfectly soft and ready to use.

To appreciate the full effect of these wonderfully satisfying cookies, you really should have a nice, cold glass of milk on the side. It's just the right thing to do.

1 cup	250 mL	raisins (divided—pay attention!)
⅓ cup	75 mL	water
½ cup	125 mL	solid vegetable shortening
1		egg
1 ½ cups	375 mL	light brown sugar
2 tsp	10 mL	vanilla
2 cups	500 mL	all-purpose flour
1 ¼ cups	300 mL	rolled oats (regular or quick, not instant)
2 tsp	10 mL	baking soda
½ tsp	2 mL	cinnamon
½ tsp	2 mL	salt

Preheat the oven to 275° F (140° C). Lightly grease two cookie sheets, or line them with parchment paper. Set aside.

In a blender or food processor, combine *half* of the raisins (listen up—*half* of them!) with the water and blend until it forms a gloppy, brown puree. Reserve the remaining raisins intact.

In a large mixing bowl, with an electric mixer, beat together the raisin puree, the vegetable shortening, egg, brown sugar and vanilla until smooth.

In another bowl, stir together the flour, oats, baking soda, cinnamon and salt. Combine this mixture with the egg mixture and beat until all the ingredients are evenly mixed. Stir in the remaining raisins (remember them?).

By hand, form the dough into golf ball–sized balls and place on a baking sheet about 2 inches (5 cm) apart. Flatten slightly to about ½-inch (1 cm) thickness. Bake for 18 to 20 minutes until lightly browned on the bottom, but still soft in the middle. Don't overbake them or they'll lose their chewiness. Let cool before indulging.

Makes 2 to 3 dozen big chewy cookies.

Tips for the Cookie-Baking Perfectionist

- Drop cookies have the irritating tendency to be unevenly shaped, odd-sized, and annoyingly imperfect. If this bothers you, chill the dough for several hours before baking to firm it up. You can then roll it by hand into identical, perfect balls and place them, in precise geometric rows, onto your cookie sheet for baking.

- Use a miniature ice cream scoop to accurately measure out your cookie dough onto the baking sheet. "Heaping teaspoon" is *such* a vague term, isn't it?

- When making slice-and-bake cookies, freeze the logs of dough before slicing so that the cylinders don't get squashed when you cut them. There—perfectly round cookies.

- When rolling out cookie dough, place two chopsticks (or some other stick of the proper thickness) on the counter to use as a "thickness" guide for your rolling pin. That way, all your cookies will be the exactly the same thickness.

Better-Than-Average Chocolate Chip Cookies

Seriously overloaded with chocolate chips, these cookies are definitely better than average. Some might say they're the best. But we're not bragging.

1 cup	250 mL	unsalted butter
½ cup	125 mL	granulated sugar
1 ½ cups	375 mL	light brown sugar
2		eggs
2 ½ tsp	12 mL	vanilla
2 ½ cups	625 mL	all-purpose flour
½ tsp	2 mL	salt
1 tsp	5 mL	baking powder
1 tsp	5 mL	baking soda
2 ½ cups	625 mL	semisweet chocolate chips

Preheat the oven to 350° F (180° C). Lightly grease two cookie sheets, or line them with parchment paper. Set aside.

In a large mixing bowl, with an electric mixer, cream together the butter, granulated sugar, brown sugar, eggs and vanilla, beating until smooth and fluffy.

In another bowl, mix together the flour, salt, baking powder and baking soda. Add this mixture to the butter mixture, beating until everything is well mixed. Stir in the chocolate chips.

By hand, form the dough into golf ball–sized balls and place them 2 inches (5 cm) apart on the cookie sheet. Bake for 9 to 10 minutes, just until the edges are beginning to brown lightly. It's better to underbake these cookies slightly, so remove them from the oven while they're still a bit soft in the middle.

Makes 2 to 3 dozen chocolate chip cookies of your dreams.

Giant Snickerdoodles

Sounds a bit like a type of enormous, extinct flightless bird, doesn't it? Well it's not. This is a great big cookie—perfect for dunking.

1 ½ cups	375 mL	granulated sugar
1 cup	250 mL	butter
2		eggs
2 ¾ cups	625 mL	all-purpose flour
2 tsp	10 mL	cream of tartar
1 tsp	5 mL	baking soda
1 tbsp	15 mL	cinnamon
3 tbsp	45 mL	granulated sugar

In a large bowl, with an electric mixer, beat together the 1 ½ cups (375 mL) sugar, butter and eggs until light and fluffy—about 5 minutes. Scrape down the sides a few times to keep things well mixed.

In another bowl, stir together the flour, cream of tartar and baking soda. Add to the butter mixture, beating until well blended. Refrigerate dough for at least half an hour (or longer) to allow it to firm up so that you can handle it.

Preheat the oven to 375° F (190° C).

In a flat bowl or pie plate, mix together the cinnamon and the 3 tbsp (45 mL) sugar. By hand, shape the dough into 2-inch (5 cm) balls (remember, these are *giant* snickerdoodles) and roll each one in the cinnamon sugar mixture until it is completely coated. Place on an ungreased baking sheet, at least 3 inches (8 cm) apart—*they will spread a lot*. Bake for 12 to 15 minutes, until cookies are firm around the edges—the middle may still be a bit soft. Remove to a rack to cool.

Makes about 2 ½ dozen giant flightless cookies.

Regular, Everyday Peanut Butter Cookies

You simply can't argue with a peanut butter cookie. It's a lunchbox classic.

½ cup	125 mL	butter
½ cup	125 mL	peanut butter
½ cup	125 mL	granulated sugar
½ cup	125 mL	light brown sugar
1		egg
1 ¼ cup	300 mL	all-purpose or whole wheat flour
½ tsp	2 mL	baking powder
½ tsp	2 mL	baking soda

Preheat the oven to 375° F (190° C).

In a large mixing bowl, using an electric mixer, beat together the butter, peanut butter, granulated and brown sugars and the egg until creamy and thoroughly mixed. Add the flour, baking powder and baking soda and blend very well. That's it for the dough.

Now make the cookies: by hand, roll the dough into 1-inch (2 cm) balls, place them on an ungreased cookie sheet, leaving 2 inches (5 cm) between them to allow for spreading. For the classic peanut butter cookie look, flatten each ball of dough with a fork, pressing lightly to make a criss-cross pattern. There—isn't that just lovely? Bake for 10 to 12 minutes, until the cookies have puffed slightly and are lightly browned on the bottom.

Makes about 3 ½ dozen.

Whole Wheat Peanut Butter Banana Cookies

The classic sandwich in cookie form. Brilliant.

1 cup	250 mL	all-purpose flour
1 cup	250 mL	whole wheat flour
2 tsp	10 mL	baking powder
1 cup	250 mL	light brown sugar
¾ cup	175 mL	peanut butter
½ cup	125 mL	butter
2		medium bananas, peeled and cut into chunks
2		eggs

Preheat the oven to 350° F (180° C). Lightly grease two cookie sheets, or line them with parchment. Set aside.

In a large bowl, stir together the all-purpose flour, whole wheat flour and baking powder. Set aside.

Into the container of a blender or food processor, place the brown sugar, peanut butter, butter, bananas and eggs. Whirl until smooth, scraping down the sides once or twice. Pour the banana mixture into the flour mixture, and stir until evenly combined into a thick batter.

Drop dough by heaping teaspoonfuls onto the cookie sheet, leaving enough room between the cookies for expansion. Bake for 12 to 15 minutes, until cookies are set and lightly browned on the bottom.

Makes 4 dozen.

Variation

Chocolate Chips? Why Not?
Add ½ cup (125 mL) semisweet chocolate chips to the batter. Go ahead. Do it.

Hermit Cookies

You don't have to be a cave-dwelling hermit to appreciate these cookies. They're also good to share with friends. In your kitchen.

½ cup	125 mL	butter
1 cup	250 mL	light brown sugar
1		egg
2 tbsp	30 mL	water
1 ½ cups	375 mL	all-purpose flour
1 tbsp	15 mL	instant coffee powder
½ tsp	2 mL	baking soda
½ tsp	2 mL	cinnamon
¼ tsp	1 mL	nutmeg
¼ tsp	1 mL	cloves
¾ cup	175 mL	raisins
½ cup	125 mL	chopped walnuts

Preheat the oven to 375° F (190° C). Grease two cookie sheets, or line them with parchment. Set aside.

In a large mixing bowl, with an electric mixer, cream together the butter and brown sugar until just mixed. Add the egg and water and continue beating until smooth. The mixture may look curdled at first, but continue beating and it should even out. If not, don't worry—it'll still be OK.

In another bowl, stir together the flour, instant coffee (crush the granules if they're too chunky), baking soda, cinnamon, nutmeg and cloves. Add this to the butter mixture and beat just until smooth. Mix in the raisins and walnuts until combined.

Drop batter, by heaping teaspoons, onto the cookie sheets, about 2 inches (5 cm) apart—they will spread. Bake for 8 to 10 minutes, until the cookies are set and the bottoms lightly browned. Remove to a rack to cool.

Makes about 3 dozen.

Soft Ginger Cookies

These ginger cookies are deliciously chewy and gingery, and you can easily eat a dozen of them before you even notice you've done it. Maybe that's not such a good thing.

¾ cup	175 mL	butter
1 cup	250 mL	granulated sugar
1		egg
1 tbsp	15 mL	water
¼ cup	50 mL	molasses
2 ¼ cups	550 mL	all-purpose flour
2 tsp	10 mL	ground ginger
1 tsp	5 mL	baking soda
1 tsp	5 mL	cinnamon
		additional granulated sugar for rolling cookies

In a large bowl, with an electric mixer, cream together the butter and sugar until fluffy. Beat in the egg, water and molasses and continue mixing until smooth.

In another bowl, stir together the flour, ginger, baking soda and cinnamon. Add this mixture to the butter mixture, and beat until everything is thoroughly combined into a soft dough. Cover with plastic wrap and refrigerate for at least 30 minutes, until the dough is firm enough to handle.

Preheat the oven to 350° F (180° C).

Dump some sugar onto a plate. By hand, roll the dough into 1 to 1 ½-inch (2.5 to 4 cm) balls, then roll each ball of dough in the sugar, turning to coat all sides. Place balls on an ungreased baking sheet, about 2 inches (5 cm) apart to allow for spreading (they really will spread). Bake for 8 to 10 minutes—now here's the thing: these cookies will be really soft and you won't think they're ready, but take them out anyway. Let them cool for a couple of minutes on the cookie sheet, then remove them to a rack to cool completely. They *will* firm up. No really, they will.

Makes 3 ½ to 4 dozen perfect, chewy ginger cookies.

Health-Nut Cookies

Yes, the ingredient list is seriously long but, let's face it, these are serious cookies. They're packed with nutrition—you could probably live on them if you had to.

1 ½ cups	375 mL	raisins, currants or dried cranberries
1 cup	250 mL	chopped walnuts
1 cup	250 mL	chopped pecans
1 cup	250 mL	peanuts
½ cup	125 mL	pine nuts
½ cup	125 mL	sunflower seeds (toasted or not)
½ cup	125 mL	sesame seeds
½ cup	125 mL	wheat germ
1 cup	250 mL	quick-cooking rolled oats (not instant)
1 cup	250 mL	whole wheat flour
2 tsp	10 mL	baking powder
1 tsp	5 mL	cinnamon
½ tsp	2 mL	ground ginger
1 cup	250 mL	butter
½ cup	125 mL	peanut butter
1 ¼ cups	300 mL	light brown sugar
2		eggs
¼ cup	50 mL	milk

Preheat the oven to 350° F (180° C). Grease two baking sheets, or line them with parchment. Set aside.

In a very large bowl, combine the raisins (or whatever), walnuts, pecans, peanuts, pine nuts, sunflower seeds, sesame seeds, wheat germ and rolled oats. Toss until well mixed.

In a small bowl, stir together the whole wheat flour, baking powder, cinnamon and ginger. Add this mixture to the fruit and nut mixture, and stir until everything is combined.

In another bowl with an electric mixer, cream together the butter, peanut butter and brown sugar until fluffy—about 5 minutes. Add the eggs and milk, and beat until thoroughly mixed. With a large wooden spoon, stir the butter mixture into the dry ingredients and mix until everything is evenly mushed together. It should be moist enough to form a thick dough.

Using a ¼-cup (50 mL) measure to scoop the dough, drop large lumps of this mixture onto the baking sheets, at least 2 inches (5 cm) apart. Bake for 16 to 18 minutes, until cookies are lightly browned on the bottom and set (but still a little soft) on top.

Makes 3 dozen big, outrageously nutritious cookies.

Now, go out hiking or something.

Chocolate Damnation Cookies

No. Stop. Don't make these.

10 squares		(1 oz/28 g each) semisweet chocolate
½ cup	125 mL	butter
1 cup	250 mL	light brown sugar
½ cup	125 mL	granulated sugar
4		eggs
1 tsp	5 mL	vanilla
2 ¼ cups	550 mL	all-purpose flour
1 tsp	5 mL	baking powder
1 tsp	5 mL	baking soda
1 tbsp	15 mL	black coffee (leftover is fine)
2 cups	500 mL	coarsely chopped semisweet chocolate (or chocolate chips)
1 cup	250 mL	coarsely chopped pecans
1 cup	250 mL	dried cranberries (optional but excellent)

Place the chocolate squares in a double boiler or a saucepan set over a pan of hot (not boiling water), and melt, stirring, until the chocolate is smooth. Remove from heat and let cool slightly while you prepare the remaining ingredients.

In a large mixing bowl, with an electric mixer, cream the butter, brown sugar, and granulated sugar, beating until smooth. Add the eggs and vanilla, and continue to beat until well blended. Beat in the melted chocolate, then fold in the flour, baking powder, baking soda and coffee. Now add the chopped chocolate (or chocolate chips), the pecans, and the cranberries and stir until everything is evenly distributed. Cover the bowl with plastic wrap and chill for about an hour to allow the dough to firm up.

Preheat the oven to 350° F (180° C). Lightly grease two cookie sheets, or line them with parchment.

Place golf ball–sized (or slightly larger) balls of dough onto the cookie sheets, about 2 inches (5 cm) apart. Bake until just set—13 to

15 minutes. These cookies are best if you undercook them slightly, so remove them from the oven while they're still a bit soft—they'll firm up as they cool.

Makes about 2 dozen bad, *bad* cookies.

Melting Chocolate

Sure, you can leave a chocolate bar in your glove compartment and it will melt. But it won't melt properly. *Here's how to do it right (and avoid messing up your road maps).*

In a Double Boiler

Place as much chocolate as you'll need, broken up into chunks, into the top section of a double boiler. Fill the bottom section with hot water and place on the stove. Bring the water to a simmer over medium heat, then turn off the heat and let the chocolate melt, stirring over the hot water, until smooth.

Without a Double Boiler

Break chocolate into chunks and place in a small saucepan. Set the saucepan into a slightly bigger saucepan or skillet. Add hot water to the bigger pan, making sure not a single drop can possibly slosh into the chocolate (it will ruin it). Bring the water to a simmer over medium heat, then turn off the heat and let the chocolate melt, stirring until smooth.

In a Microwave

Chop your chocolate squares into chunks and place in a microwave-safe bowl. Microwave on medium power for 2 to 3 minutes (for two squares), stirring once partway through. Increase the amount of time (30 seconds at a time) for more chocolate. Watch carefully so that the chocolate doesn't burn.

Chocolate Crinkles

Chocolate sparkle variation

Roll the balls of dough in granulated sugar instead of icing sugar for a sparkly, if somewhat less dramatic looking, cookie.

These cookies look like the aftermath of a horrible natural disaster. A drought. An earthquake. Too depressing. Don't think about it. Have a cookie.

½ cup	125 mL	vegetable oil
4 squares		(1 oz/28 g each) unsweetened chocolate
2 cups	500 mL	granulated sugar
4		eggs
2 tsp	10 mL	vanilla
2 cups	500 mL	all-purpose flour
2 tsp	10 mL	baking powder
1 cup	250 mL	icing sugar

In a small saucepan, heat the oil and chocolate over low heat, stirring until the chocolate is melted and the mixture is smooth. Transfer to a mixing bowl. Add the sugar, eggs and vanilla, and beat with an electric mixer until smooth and well blended. Mix in the flour and baking powder, and beat just until the flour is incorporated into the dough. Chill in the refrigerator for at least several hours or overnight.

Preheat the oven to 350° F (180° F). Lightly grease two baking sheets, or line them with parchment paper.

Sift the icing sugar into a flat bowl or pie plate. By hand, form the dough into 1-inch (2 cm) balls and roll in the icing sugar until completely coated. Place on the baking sheets, at least 1 ½ inches (4 cm) apart. Bake for 10 to 12 minutes, until the cookies are puffed and crackled, but still slightly soft in the center. Remove to a rack to cool.

Makes 5 ½ to 6 dozen dramatically crinkled cookies.

Lacy Almond Crisps

These pretty cookies are really fun to watch as they bake. Just be careful not to let them burn—the baking time is very short.

6 tbsp	90 mL	butter
⅓ cup	75 mL	light brown sugar
3 tbsp	45 mL	corn syrup
¾ cup	175 mL	finely ground almonds
⅓ cup	75 mL	all-purpose flour
1 tsp	5 mL	vanilla
½ cup	125 mL	semisweet chocolate chips, melted (optional but excellent)

Preheat the oven to 350° F (180° C). Line a cookie sheet with parchment paper. (You can use foil if you don't have parchment—but parchment really is better.)

In a medium saucepan, combine butter, brown sugar and corn syrup. Bring to a boil, stirring, over medium heat. Remove from heat and stir in almonds, flour and vanilla. Mix well.

Drop batter by little half-teaspoonfuls, 3 inches (8 cm) apart onto the paper-lined cookie sheet. Yes, it's just a tiny bit of dough—trust me, it's magic.

Bake for 5 to 7 minutes until the cookies turn golden and stop bubbling (watch them through the oven window if you have one). Let cookies cool on the baking sheet for a couple of minutes before carefully sliding them onto a rack to cool completely.

Drizzle the cooled cookies with melted semisweet chocolate (oh—to die for) or leave them plain.

Makes about 5 dozen indescribably delicious cookies that will disappear instantly.

Almost Authentic Scottish Shortbread

You don't have to go all the way to Loch Ness to get Scottish short-bread cookies. Unless, of course, you want to.

1 cup	250 mL	unsalted butter (don't even *think* about using margarine)
½ cup	125 mL	icing sugar
2 cups	500 mL	all-purpose flour
		pinch of salt

Preheat the oven to 300° F (150° C).

In a large bowl with an electric mixer (or in a food processor), beat together the butter and the icing sugar until well blended. Add the flour and salt and blend into a smooth dough. Wrap dough in plastic wrap and refrigerate for 30 minutes to 1 hour. If you chill it any longer than that, the dough will harden and be difficult to shape. (You'll have to leave it out at room temperature to soften up again.)

Roll the dough into 1-inch (2 cm) balls, place them on an ungreased cookie sheet and flatten very slightly (to about ½-inch/ 1 cm thickness) with the bottom of a glass that has been dipped in flour to prevent sticking. Prick a few fork holes in each cookie before baking to make them look more authentic.

Or you can squish the dough evenly into an ungreased square 9-inch (23 cm) baking pan. Poke all over with a fork.

Bake for 45 minutes for a square pan, 25 to 30 minutes for individual cookies. The square pan of shortbread should be allowed to cool completely before carefully cutting into small squares with a very sharp knife.

Makes about 2 ½ to 3 dozen almost authentic shortbread cookies.

Three Inauthentic (but Genuinely Delicious) Shortbread Variations

There are those who might object to taking liberties with something as sacred as Scottish shortbread. And then again, there are those who wouldn't object at all.

Chocolate Chunk Shortbread

Add 1 cup (250 mL) coarsely chopped semisweet (or bittersweet or milk) chocolate to the dough before chilling. Or use chocolate chips (if you must). Shape into balls, flatten slightly (as above) and bake as if it were normal shortbread. Deadly.

Lemon or Orange Shortbread

Add 1 tbsp (15 mL) finely grated lemon or orange peel to the dough before chilling. Shape and bake as above.

Butter Pecan Shortbread

Omit icing sugar from the basic recipe and use light brown sugar instead. Add 1 cup (250 mL) ground pecans and 2 tsp (10 mL) vanilla along with the flour. Shape and bake as above.

Plain and Simple Sugar Cookies

But they're too plain!

- Brush unbaked cookies with beaten egg white and sprinkle with plain or colored sugar before baking.

- Decorate baked cookies with Royal Decorator Icing (see page 167).

- Glaze baked cookies with Shiny Sugar Glaze (see page 167) or Chocolate Ganache Glaze (page 166). Add sprinkles (if you must) while the glaze is still wet.

- Or glaze each cookie, half and half for a classic New York Black and White.

- Mix a few drops of liquid or paste food coloring into a beaten egg yolk and paint lovely designs on plain sugar cookies *before* baking.

Cut out great big circles of dough using an empty coffee can and sprinkle with sugar before baking for the ultimate in simple cookiness. Or cut into fancy shapes (don't forget a hanging hole) to bake and hang on your Christmas tree. Suit yourself. They're your cookies now.

1 cup	250 mL	butter, softened
1 ½ cups	375 mL	granulated sugar
2		eggs
1 tsp	10 mL	vanilla
4 cups	1 liter	all-purpose flour
1 tbsp	15 mL	baking powder
¼ cup	50 mL	evaporated milk (or light cream)

In a large bowl, with an electric mixer, cream together the butter and the sugar until smooth. Add the eggs and vanilla, and continue beating until creamy. Stir in the flour and baking powder alternately with the evaporated milk to make a fairly stiff dough. Turn the dough out onto a lightly floured surface and knead a few times by hand to make it smooth and workable. Refrigerate for at least 10 minutes before using.

Preheat the oven to 350° F (180° C). Grease two baking sheets, or line them with parchment.

Cut the dough into four pieces. Working with one piece of dough at a time, roll it out on a lightly floured surface to an even ¼-inch (6 mm) thickness, dusting lightly with flour to keep it from sticking to the rolling pin. Cut out shapes with cookie cutters and place them on the baking sheets, at least 1 inch (2.5 cm) apart to allow for spreading. Bake for 13 to 15 minutes, until the cookies are very slightly browned on the bottom, but still light on top.

Makes 3 to 4 dozen cookies, depending on what sizes you make.

Gingerbread People

Is there a more cheerful way to spend a cold winter afternoon than making a colony of gingerbread people? And it doesn't have to be just people, either. Remember: dumptrucks can be festive too.

1		egg
½ cup	125 mL	molasses
1 cup	250 mL	granulated sugar
½ cup	125 mL	solid vegetable shortening, melted (not butter or margarine)
1 ½ tsp	7 mL	baking soda
2 ½ cups	625 mL	all-purpose flour
¼ tsp	1 mL	ground ginger
1 tsp	5 mL	cinnamon

In a large bowl, mix together the egg, molasses, sugar, melted shortening and baking soda. Beat well.

In another bowl, stir together the flour, ginger and cinnamon. Add the flour mixture gradually to the egg mixture, blending well. Chill the dough for several hours or overnight.

When you're ready to bake, preheat the oven to 350° F (180° C). Lightly grease two cookie sheets, or line them with parchment.

Cut the dough into 4 pieces. Form each portion into a nice compact ball, flouring it well. Roll out each piece on a well-floured surface to about ⅛-inch (3 mm) thickness.

Using cookie cutters or your own original cardboard pattern, cut out gingerbread people (or animals, or dumptrucks or whatchamacallits). Carefully transfer the people (etc.) to the cookie sheets and bake for 5 to 7 minutes—until very lightly browned around the edges. Watch them closely—small shapes will bake more quickly than large ones.

Let your cookies cool for a minute or two before removing them to a rack to cool completely. Decorate with Royal Decorator Icing (see page 167).

Makes a *lot* of people (animals, aliens, dumptrucks, etc.) or one phenomenal gingerbread house (see page 100).

Gingerbread House

Melted Sugar Glue

Measure about 1 cup (250 mL) of granulated sugar into a heavy skillet. Place over medium heat and cook, stirring occasionally, until the sugar melts and liquefies—about 5 to 10 minutes. Reduce the heat to ultra-low to keep the sugar glue liquefied throughout the construction process. It will have the consistency of honey when hot but will thicken quickly as it cools. Watch closely to avoid burning, and be careful handling it because it is screamingly hot.

Start with a batch of the same dough that you used for Gingerbread People—but this time you're making building materials. No really—it'll be fun.

You'll need the following:
1 recipe Gingerbread People dough (see page 99)
1 recipe Royal Decorator Icing (see page 167)
12-inch (30 cm) square slab of styrofoam, ½ inch (1 cm) thick
Melted sugar glue (see sidebar this page)
Cardboard Gingerbread House pattern (see page 102)
Toothpicks
Decorating stuff galore: candies, pretzels, cereal, licorice, gumdrops, etc.

Phase One: Bake the Pieces

Follow the directions for making Gingerbread People, but instead of cutting the rolled dough out into, well, *people* shapes, cut around the cardboard Gingerbread House pattern pieces to make house sections. The recipe makes enough for all the house pieces, plus an extra roof, front and side. Because, well, accidents can happen. Transfer pieces to the baking sheet very carefully, so as not to warp them (use a wide spatula or cardboard pattern to help lift the unbaked cutouts).

Bake pieces as for Gingerbread People, then cool completely.

Phase Two: Construction

Have a few toothpicks ready (these will be used for temporary support, if necessary), as well as the styrofoam base and a batch of melted sugar glue. OK, let's begin.

Working as quickly as possible, dip the bottom and side edges of one house wall into the melted sugar and place it upright in position on the styrofoam base. Do the same with the adjoining piece, making sure it sticks together at the corner. Repeat until you have the four walls standing upright. Now the roof: coat the top edges of the house walls with sugar glue and stick one roof piece in place. Do the same with the other roof section, securing them together with dabs of

The Clueless Baker

melted sugar along the top. Don't worry about drips—they're edible—and besides, you can hide them with icing later. Assemble the chimney, hang the door and shutters, pour yourself a cup of coffee (or whatever) and take a breather. The worst is over.

Phase Three: Decoration

Now, far be it from me to try to tell you how to decorate this fabulous creation, but perhaps I could offer some suggestions.

- Use Royal Decorator Icing to decorate the house and to stick on candies or whatever else you're using.
- Royal Decorator Icing can also be dripped from the edge of the roof to make realistic icicles.
- Pretzel sticks make good fences and cool trees.
- Marshmallows make very convincing snowmen.
- Shredded wheat cereal can be used to create a charming thatched roof.
- Chewy, green spearmint leaf-shaped candies are handy for landscaping.
- You can make cotton smoke curls for the chimney, of course.

Advanced Gingerbread-Building Techniques

Too conventional, you say? Not *creative* enough for you? Too—ack!—*suburbia*?

Well, smartypants, here's a challenge for you. Next time, try baking an assortment of "lumber" (rather than house shapes). You know—two-by-fours, planks, small sections of "drywall," doors—the kind of thing you'd get at Home Depot. Only edible. Then, with a rough plan in mind, use these pieces to spontaneously build your gingerbread creation. (Sort of like the way that moron you hired built your garage five years ago.)

Try building a treehouse, using a real branch mounted on a wooden base for a "tree," with a rope ladder (string and pretzels) leading to the ground. Or make a rustic cabin, complete with front porch and outhouse. Whatever.

Have fun building—but don't forget to eat it. Because next year, you'll make an even better one.

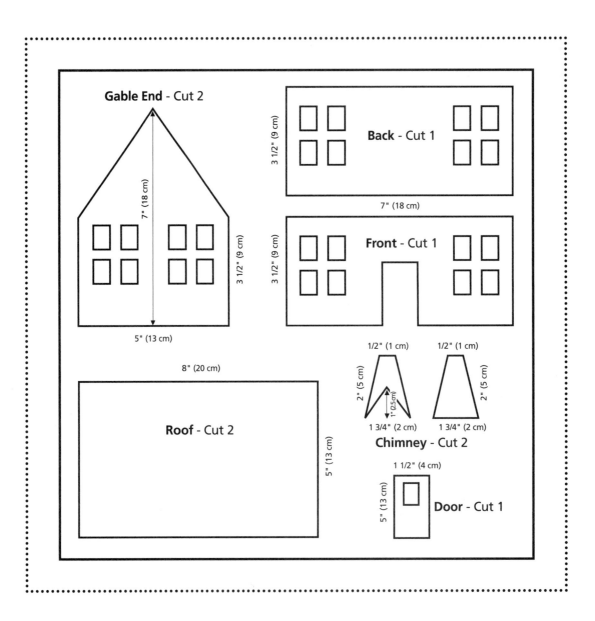

Gable End - Cut 2

7" (18 cm)

3 1/2" (9 cm)

5" (13 cm)

Back - Cut 1

3 1/2" (9 cm)

7" (18 cm)

Front - Cut 1

3 1/2" (9 cm)

8" (20 cm)

Roof - Cut 2

5" (13 cm)

1/2" (1 cm)   1/2" (1 cm)

2" (5 cm)   1" (2.5 cm)   2" (5 cm)

1 3/4" (2 cm)   1 3/4" (2 cm)

Chimney - Cut 2

1 1/2" (4 cm)

5" (13 cm)

Door - Cut 1

The Clueless Baker

Four-Way Slice and Bake Cookies

This cookie is perfect for the indecisive person with sudden cookie cravings. Ready whenever you are—keep a log or two in the freezer at all times.

1 cup	250 mL	butter
½ cup	125 mL	granulated sugar
½ cup	125 mL	light brown sugar
1		egg
1 tsp	5 mL	vanilla extract
2 cups	500 mL	all-purpose flour
½ tsp	2 mL	baking soda

So many possibilities (choose up to four ingredients)

¼ cup	50 mL	chopped raisins
¼ cup	50 mL	chopped dried cranberries
¼ cup	50 mL	chopped pecans or walnuts
¼ cup	50 mL	chocolate sprinkles
¼ cup	50 mL	colored sprinkles
¼ cup	50 mL	shredded coconut
1 square		(1 oz/28 g) semisweet chocolate, melted

In a large bowl, with an electric mixer, beat together the butter and granulated and brown sugars until creamy. Beat in the egg and the vanilla. Add the flour and the baking soda, and mix thoroughly to form a soft dough.

Divide the dough into 4 equal portions. Into *each* portion, add *one* of the above possibilities, mixing until it is evenly blended into the dough. *Or* you can simply add *one* flavoring ingredient to the entire batch of dough—just multiply by four the amount of whatever you're adding. *Or* make it half one kind and half another (you do the math). And, of course, you can always just leave the dough plain.

Shape each portion of dough into a log approximately 1 ½ inches (4 cm) thick, then wrap it in waxed paper and refrigerate or freeze for at least several hours or overnight.

When you're ready to bake the cookies, preheat the oven to 375° F (190° C).

Unwrap each log and, with a very sharp knife, slice it into ¼-inch (6 mm) thick rounds. Place slices on an ungreased baking sheet and bake for 8 to 10 minutes, until lightly browned around the edges. Remove to a rack to cool.

Makes 5 ½ to 6 dozen cookies.

The Clueless Baker

Giant Cookie Pizza

*Here's a great thing to make with a bunch of kids (or, ahem, adults)
on a rainy afternoon. Hold the pepperoni. Hold the mushrooms. And,
definitely, hold the anchovies.*

1 cup	250 mL	butter
½ cup	125 mL	granulated sugar
½ cup	125 mL	light brown sugar
1		egg
1 tsp	5 mL	vanilla
1 ¾ cups	425 mL	all-purpose flour
1 cup	250 mL	semisweet chocolate chips
1 cup	250 mL	miniature marshmallows
1 cup	250 mL	peanuts or coarsely chopped walnuts

Preheat the oven to 375° F (190° C).

In a large bowl, with an electric mixer, cream together the butter,
granulated and brown sugars, and egg and vanilla. Beat this mixture
until fluffy. Add the flour, and beat until dough is smooth.

Dump the dough out onto an ungreased 14-inch (35 cm) pizza
pan, and spread it out smoothly with a spatula, right to the edges of
the pan. Bake for 12 minutes.

Now remove this partially baked crust from the oven and sprinkle
evenly with chocolate chips, marshmallows and nuts, leaving a naked
border around the edge—for a realistic pizza effect. You might want
to try other toppings too—gumdrops, shredded coconut, whatever—
but keep the total amount of toppings to 3 cups (750 mL).

Return the pizza to the oven and bake for another 6 to 8 minutes,
until the marshmallows are lightly browned. Let cool (at least partly,
anyway) before cutting into wedges and serving.

Makes one 14-inch (35 cm) pizza.

Hamantaschen

Traditional Jewish holiday cookies, these are incredibly easy to make and really delicious. Fill them with any kind of jam or fruit filling, or stuff them with chocolate chips. Or make some of everything.

1		medium seedless orange
2		eggs
¾ cup	175 mL	granulated sugar
½ cup	125 mL	vegetable oil
2 tsp	10 mL	baking powder
2 ¾ cups	675 mL	all-purpose flour
		jam, canned pie filling or chocolate chips

Preheat the oven to 350° F (180° C). Grease two cookie sheets, or line them with parchment. Set aside.

Cut the orange into quarters—peel and all—and place it in the container of a food processor. Yes, you really need to use a food processor to make this. Blend until the orange is finely chopped. Add the eggs, sugar and oil, and process for about 10 seconds. Scrape down the sides of the container, add the baking powder and flour and process just until the flour is blended into dough. It will be soft and sticky, but that's OK.

Divide the dough into 2 or 3 portions. Roll each portion out on a well-floured board to about ⅛-inch (3 mm) thickness. Using a 3-inch (7 cm) round cookie cutter (or a glass or whatever you have handy) cut the dough into circles. (Gather up the scraps and re-roll them until you've used up all the dough.)

In the middle of each circle, put about ½ teaspoon (2 mL) of jam. Pinch the edge of each circle firmly together in three places, making a triangular enclosure with the top slightly open so that the filling peeks out. Be sure the corners are tightly pinched to avoid unsightly leakage.

Place the hamantaschen on the cookie sheets and bake for 20 to 25 minutes, or until lightly browned.

Makes about 4 dozen.

Elegant Hazelnut Raspberry Sandwich Cookies

These are not your average cookies. They are delicate and sophisti-cated. Aunt Edna would be so impressed—she didn't think you had it in you.

1 cup	250 mL	butter
½ cup	125 mL	granulated sugar
2 cups	500 mL	finely ground hazelnuts
2 cups	500 mL	all-purpose flour
1 cup	250 mL	raspberry jam
1		recipe Shiny Sugar Glaze, lemon version (see page 167)

In a mixing bowl, cream together the butter and sugar until fluffy. Beat in the ground hazelnuts and the flour, mixing until smooth. Refrigerate the dough, covered with plastic wrap, for about 30 minutes.

Preheat the oven to 350° F (180° C).

Cut the dough into 4 pieces. On a lightly floured surface, roll 1 piece at a time out to about ¼-inch (6 mm) thickness. This dough can be crumbly, so you may have to knead it a bit by hand to make it pliable enough to roll out properly. Cut with a small round cookie cutter (no bigger than 1 ½ inches/4 cm in diameter) and place on an ungreased baking sheet. Bake for 10 to 12 minutes, until lightly browned on the bottom. Let cook for a few minutes before removing from the baking sheet.

To assemble the cookie sandwiches, spread a thin layer of raspberry jam on one cookie, and top with a second one. Drizzle with Shiny Sugar Glaze—the lemon version. Let glaze dry before serving. With a cup of tea, of course.

Makes 2 to 3 dozen cookie sandwiches.

Chocolate Walnut Rugelach

These are halfway between a cookie and a pastry. They look like a lot more work than they actually are. Fun to make.

¼ cup	125 mL	granulated sugar
½ tsp	2 mL	cinnamon
⅓ cup	75 mL	chocolate chips
⅓ cup	75 mL	walnuts
1 recipe		Rich Cream Cheese Pastry (see page 174)
		icing sugar for dusting

Preheat the oven to 350° F (180° C).

In the container of a food processor, combine the sugar, cinnamon, chocolate chips and walnuts and process until finely chopped. (You can also do this in a blender—just make sure you stop and scrape the sides down several times so that everything is evenly ground.)

Cut the ball of pastry dough into 4 pieces, and dust each lightly with flour. With a rolling pin on a lightly floured surface, roll out one ball of dough into a circle approximately 10 inches (25 cm) in diameter. Handle the dough gently, and don't be afraid to dust it with more flour to prevent the dough from sticking to the counter or the rolling pin. Now sprinkle the entire surface of this circle evenly with ¼ of the filling. Using a pizza cutter (or a sharp knife), cut the circle into 8 wedges—pizza-style. Roll each wedge up—*starting at the wide, outside edge*—rolling firmly toward the point. Place on an ungreased cookie sheet and bend each one slightly to form a crescent. There—aren't they cute? Repeat with the rest of the dough and filling.

Bake for 15 to 20 minutes, until very lightly browned on top, and browned, but not burnt, on the bottom. Remove to a rack to cool, then dust with icing sugar before serving.

Makes exactly 32 rugelach.

Dog Biscuits

Thoroughly dog-tested and deemed to be woof-worthy by our panel of canine experts. Tastes almost as good as week-old dead groundhog. Or so we've been told.

3 cups	750 mL	whole wheat flour
2 cups	500 mL	quick-cooking rolled oats (not instant)
¼ cup	50 mL	wheat germ
¼ cup	50 mL	skim milk powder
½ tsp	2 mL	garlic powder
1 ¼ cups	300 mL	water
⅓ cup	75 mL	peanut butter
1		egg

Preheat oven to 275° F (140° C). Lightly grease two cookie sheets, or line them with parchment. Set aside.

In a large bowl, mix together the flour, oats, wheat germ, powdered milk and garlic powder.

In the container of a blender or food processor, blend the water, peanut butter and egg until smooth. Stir this liquid mixture into the flour mixture to form a stiff dough.

Roll this dough out onto a floured surface to about ½-inch (1 cm) thickness (the biscuits are supposed to be chunky) and cut into shapes with cookie cutters. Dog bone–shaped cookie cutters would be a logical choice, but your dog may prefer letter carriers or, uh, cats. Place on the cookie sheets, and bake for 1 ½ to 2 hours. (Yes, that's right— 1 ½ to 2 hours. They should be very hard and crunchy.)

Makes 3 to 4 dozen.

Nonedible Cookies

Interesting effect

Work some concentrated paste (not liquid) food coloring into the dough before rolling it out. If you knead it in with your hands, you can get a really neat marbleized effect. You can find paste food coloring in any store that sells serious cake decorating supplies. It's superconcentrated and produces really vibrant colors. (The stuff is great for tinting frosting too.)

So you're thinking…what's the point, right? Well, for one thing, this stuff makes really cool Christmas tree decorations. Spray paint them silver or gold. Decorate them with water-based paint and coat them with urethane. Or just go crazy with glitter and glue and whatever you can find. This is art—we don't need a point.

2 cups	500 mL	all-purpose flour
1 cup	250 mL	salt
1 cup	250 mL	water

Preheat the oven to 250° F (120° C). Lightly grease two baking sheets, or line them with parchment. Set aside.

In a bowl, combine the flour and salt and mix well. Add water gradually, stirring, until the dough forms a ball and is easy to handle. You may not need to add all the water if the dough seems soft enough, so don't dump all the water in at once. Knead the dough on a lightly floured surface until smooth—about 5 minutes or so.

Roll the dough out about ¼-inch/6 mm thick on a lightly floured surface. Cut into shapes with cookie cutters (or whatever you want) and place on the baking sheets. Bake for 35 to 40 minutes, until the, um, thingamabobs are firm and dry. Let cool, then decorate them in whatever wild and wonderful way you like.

Makes about 25 medium shapes, and they last practically forever. Which is a good thing because they are, after all, art.

Squares and Bars

Easy Saucepan Brownies

Here's a good basic brownie that's delicious—and ridiculously easy to make. Sprinkle with icing sugar for a simple finishing touch. Or spread with chocolate frosting for a more serious chocolate impact.

⅓ cup	75 mL	butter
⅔ cup	150 mL	granulated sugar
1 cup	250 mL	semisweet chocolate chips
2 tbsp	30 mL	water
2		eggs
¾ cup	175 mL	all-purpose flour
½ tsp	2 mL	baking powder
1 tsp	5 mL	vanilla
½ cup	125 mL	coarsely chopped walnuts (optional)

Preheat the oven to 350° F (180° C). Grease an 8-inch (20 cm) square baking pan. Set aside.

In a medium saucepan, combine the butter, sugar, chocolate chips and water. Place over low heat and cook, stirring constantly, just until the chocolate is melted and the mixture is smooth. Remove from heat and let cool for a couple of minutes.

Add the eggs to the chocolate mixture and whisk until smooth. Dump in the flour, baking powder and vanilla, stirring just until the dry ingredients have been incorporated, then add the chopped walnuts and stir to mix. Pour into the prepared baking pan, and bake for 25 to 30 minutes—until a toothpick poked into the middle comes out nearly clean. If you're not quite sure, then they're done.

Makes 20 to 25 brownies.

Two-Bite Brownies

Use this recipe to make a batch of little weensy individual brownies just like the ones they sell in bags at the supermarket. Better, actually. Warning: They're seriously addictive.

Prepare Easy Saucepan Brownie batter, but omit the nuts. Spoon the batter into well-greased miniature muffin pans (1 heaping teaspoon in each cup). Bake at 350° F (180° C) for 10 to 12 minutes.

Makes about 48 individual brownies.

Dastardly Double Fudge Brownies

Ack! I wrecked my chocolate!

Did you splash water into the chocolate you were melting? And now you're sorry—it's all seized up into icky, clumpy bits that will not go away. Disaster? Well, maybe not. Here's how you may still be able to rescue your ruined chocolate.

For each 1-oz (28 g) square of chocolate (or equivalent amount of chocolate chips) that has been tragically wrecked, add 1 tsp (5 mL) vegetable oil or solid vegetable shortening, and place back over hot water, stirring until smooth. Don't use butter or margarine because they contain water and will only make matters worse.

And be more careful next time, will you please?

These brownies are thick and fudgy and positively dastardly. They really need no frosting, but if you insist, you can slather them with Chocolate Ganache Glaze (see page 166) or Creamy Chocolate Frosting (see page 162) when they're completely cool. Like they'll last that long.

4 squares		(1 oz/28 g each) unsweetened chocolate
¾ cup	175 mL	butter
1 ½ cups	375 mL	granulated sugar
3		eggs
2 tsp	10 mL	vanilla
¾ cup	175 mL	all-purpose flour
½ cup	125 mL	semisweet chocolate chips
½ cup	125 mL	chopped walnuts (optional)

Preheat the oven to 350° F (180° C). Grease an 8-inch (20 cm) square baking pan. Set aside.

In a medium-sized saucepan melt together the chocolate and the butter over low heat, stirring occasionally until the mixture is smooth. Remove from heat and let cool slightly.

With a whisk (or an electric mixer on low speed) beat in the sugar, then add the eggs and vanilla, and continue beating until smooth. Stir in the flour, mixing just until it disappears into the batter, then add the chocolate chips and walnuts (if you're using them). Mix well and pour into the prepared baking pan. Bake for 35 to 40 minutes, until set but not dry (a toothpick poked into the middle of the pan should come out with a little bit of stuff clinging to it). Don't overbake—it will ruin the fudgy effect.

Makes 25 utterly dastardly brownies.

Marbled Peanut Butter Brownies

There's chocolate. And there's peanut butter. Together. In one brownie. You're doomed.

½ cup	125 mL	butter
¼ cup	50 mL	peanut butter
1 tsp	5 mL	vanilla
1 cup	250 mL	granulated sugar
1 cup	250 mL	light brown sugar
3		eggs
2 cups	500 mL	all-purpose flour
2 tsp	10 mL	baking powder
½ cup	125 mL	chocolate syrup (the regular chocolate milk kind)

Preheat the oven to 350° F (180° C). Grease a 9 x 13-inch (23 x 33 cm) baking pan. Set aside.

In a large bowl, cream together the butter, peanut butter and vanilla with an electric mixer until blended. Add the granulated and brown sugars, and then the eggs, one at a time, beating the mixture until fluffy.

In another bowl, stir together the flour and the baking powder. Add this to the peanut butter mixture, mix well.

Now, spread half of the batter in the prepared baking pan. Drizzle the chocolate syrup over the batter, then top with the remaining batter. (The top layer of batter may not spread easily over the chocolate syrup. Just glop it on as well as you can—it'll be fine, you'll see.) Swirl the mixture by running a knife through the batter several times to create a marbled effect. Don't overswirl—you wouldn't want to ruin the marbled effect. Bake for 35 to 40 minutes, until lightly browned.

Let cool before cutting into squares.

Makes about 36 swirly brownies.

Butterscotch Granola Blondies

Use whatever kind of granola you happen to have to make these chewy, delicious bars. They're even good with stale, leftover stuff from the bottom of the box.

¼ cup	50 mL	vegetable oil
1 cup	250 mL	light brown sugar
1		egg
2 tsp	10 mL	vanilla
¾ cup	175 mL	all-purpose flour
1 tsp	5 mL	baking powder
1 cup	250 mL	granola cereal (any kind)

Preheat the oven to 350° F (180° C). Grease an 8-inch (20 cm) square baking pan. Set aside.

In a medium bowl, combine the oil, brown sugar, egg and vanilla. Beat until well mixed. Add the flour, baking powder and granola and stir just until the dry ingredients have been incorporated into the batter. It will be thick.

Spread batter in the prepared baking pan and bake for 25 to 30 minutes. Cut into squares while still warm.

Makes 25 blondies.

Chocolate Hazelnut Truffle Squares

These squares are brownies with delusions of grandeur. Dense and outrageous, they should be cut into teensy squares for serving.

6 tbsp	90 mL	butter
2 squares		(1 oz/28 g each) unsweetened chocolate
1 cup	250 mL	granulated sugar
3		eggs
2 tsp	10 mL	vanilla
1 ½ cups	375 mL	finely ground hazelnuts

Preheat oven to 325° F (160° C). Grease an 8-inch (20 cm) square baking pan. Set aside.

In a medium saucepan, melt together the butter and the chocolate over low heat, stirring until smooth. Remove from heat and stir in the sugar, eggs and vanilla. Beat with an electric mixer or whisk until blended, then stir in the hazelnuts. Mix thoroughly and spread batter evenly into the prepared baking pan. Bake for 40 to 45 minutes, until set, and a toothpick poked into the middle of the dish comes out more or less clean.

Let cool completely before cutting into tiny little squares, then store in the refrigerator.

Makes 36 outrageously rich squares. Don't even *think* of having more than one.

Survival Bars

Don't you just hate it when you get lost in the jungle? Well, at least you won't starve if you remembered to pack a few of these in your knapsack. Also good for less dire (but equally stressful) situations—like school lunchboxes.

	3		eggs
	¾ cup	175 mL	granulated sugar
	¾ cup	175 mL	whole wheat flour
	¼ cup	50 mL	wheat germ
	1 cup	250 mL	semisweet chocolate chips
	1 cup	250 mL	chopped walnuts
	1 cup	250 mL	shredded coconut
	1 cup	250 mL	chopped dates

(handwritten notes:) ½c white & brown / Soy protein / P.B. chips / 1½c Nutmix / 1½c fruitmix

Preheat the oven to 350° F (180° C). Grease an 8-inch (20 cm) square baking pan. Set aside.

In a large bowl, with an electric mixer, beat the eggs with the sugar for 2 or 3 minutes, until well beaten and light. Stir in the flour and the wheat germ, then add the chocolate chips, walnuts, coconut and dates. Mix well and pour into the prepared baking pan. Bake for 25 to 30 minutes, until lightly browned on the edges.

Let cool completely before cutting into bars with a very sharp knife.

Makes 18 to 20 survival bars. Will keep you alive for a couple of days, at least.

Zingy Lemon Squares

What we have here is a serious lemon hit. Perfect (perfect!) with a cup of tea, these are elegant and irresistible. Don't forget to dust the top with icing sugar.

Base

2 cups	500 mL	all-purpose flour
1 cup	250 mL	unsalted butter
½ cup	125 mL	icing sugar

Topping

4		eggs
2 cups	500 mL	granulated sugar
6 tbsp	90 mL	lemon juice (approximately the juice of 2 lemons)
		grated zest from 2 lemons
¼ cup	50 mL	all-purpose flour
1 tsp	5 mL	baking powder
		additional icing sugar for sprinkling on top

Nuke that lemon

To get maximum juice from your lemon, zap it in the microwave for 10 seconds on high power before squeezing. The lemon will be easier to squeeze, and you'll get more juice. Just another one of life's little mysteries.

Preheat the oven to 350° F (180° C). Grease a 9 x 13-inch (23 x 33 cm) baking pan. Set aside.

In a medium bowl, with a pastry blender, combine the flour, butter and icing sugar, mixing them together into a crumbly mixture (don't worry about getting it to stick together). Press this mixture evenly into the bottom of the prepared baking pan. Bake for 20 minutes—just until the crust begins to set.

For the topping, beat together the eggs, granulated sugar, lemon juice and zest. Add the flour and baking powder and beat until smooth. Pour over the hot base and return the pan to the oven. Bake for another 25 minutes, until the topping is set and very lightly browned. Let cool completely, then sprinkle with icing sugar from a strainer, and cut into squares.

Makes about 28 squares.

Butter Tart Squares Variation

Use the same base recipe as for the Zingy Lemon Squares (see page 117), but substitute the following topping to make a batch of incredibly gooey and delicious butter tart squares.

2 ¼ cups	550 mL	light brown sugar
6 tbsp	90 mL	melted butter
3		eggs
2 tbsp	30 mL	vinegar
2 tsp	10 mL	vanilla
1 cup	250 mL	raisins or chopped walnuts

Preheat the oven to 350° F (180° C).

Beat together the brown sugar, melted butter, eggs, vinegar and vanilla until blended. Sprinkle the raisins (or nuts) evenly over the partially baked base, then pour the brown sugar mixture over top. Bake for 25 to 30 minutes, until set. Let cool completely before cutting into squares.

Makes 28 squares.

Coconutty Squares Variation

Same Zingy Lemon Square base—different topping.

3		eggs
2 cups	500 mL	light brown sugar
3 tbsp	45 mL	all-purpose flour
2 tsp	10 mL	baking powder
1 ½ cups	375 mL	chopped walnuts
1 ½ cups	375 mL	unsweetened shredded coconut

Preheat the oven to 350° F (180° C).

In a large bowl with an electric mixer, beat together the eggs and the brown sugar for about 5 minutes, until thickened. Stir in the flour and baking powder, mix well. Add the walnuts and coconut and stir to combine. Pour over partially baked, base and bake for 30 to 35 minutes, or until set. Cut into squares while still warm.

Makes 28 squares.

Crumbly Apple Squares

These are delicious old-timey squares that will crumble all over your lap if you try to eat them while driving your car.

1 ½ cups	375 mL	all-purpose flour
1 ½ cups	375 mL	quick-cooking rolled oats (not instant)
½ cup	125 mL	light brown sugar
¾ cup	175 mL	butter
4		medium apples, peeled, cored and thinly sliced
2 tbsp	30 mL	granulated sugar
1 tsp	5 mL	lemon juice
½ tsp	2 mL	cinnamon

Preheat the oven to 350° F (180° C). Lightly grease an 8 or 9-inch (23 or 33 cm) square baking pan. Set aside.

In a medium bowl, mix together the flour, oats and brown sugar. Using a pastry blender (or even just a fork) cut the butter into the flour mixture, mashing it up into a crumbly mixture. You don't have to worry about being delicate here—just smush the butter into the dry ingredients until it disappears. Dump most of this mixture (about two-thirds of it) into the prepared baking pan. Press down to form an even layer. Set aside the remaining crumbs.

In another bowl, toss together the sliced apples (there should be about 4 cups/1 liter), the sugar, lemon juice and cinnamon. Spread over the crumbly mixture in the pan, patting it down to eliminate any spaces. Cover with the remaining crumble mixture, pressing firmly over the apples.

Bake for 45 to 50 minutes, until the squares are lightly browned around the edges, and the apples feel soft when you (inconspicuously) poke into them with a knife.

Let cool for at least 10 minutes before cutting into squares and serving with ice cream. But they're also delicious served cold.

Makes about 25 squares.

Jam Squares

Instead of the apple filling, spread 1 ½ cups (375 mL) of any type of jam (even weird leftover stuff) over the bottom crust, then proceed with the recipe as usual. Reduce the baking time to 30 to 35 minutes.

Cheesecake Squares

You want a little cheesecake. But not too much. So here. Make these.

⅓ cup	75 mL	butter
⅓ cup	75 mL	light brown sugar
1 cup	250 mL	all-purpose flour
½ cup	125 mL	chopped pecans
8 oz	250 g	cream cheese, softened
¼ cup	50 mL	granulated sugar
1		egg
1 tbsp	15 mL	lemon juice
1 tsp	5 mL	vanilla

Preheat the oven to 350° F (180° C).

In a mixing bowl, cream together the butter and brown sugar until fluffy. Add the flour and pecans, stirring until it forms a crumbly mixture. Press half of the crumbs into the bottom of an ungreased 8-inch (20 cm) square baking pan. (Set aside the remaining crumbs for later.) Bake the crust for 12 to 14 minutes—until just beginning to set at the edges. Remove from the oven and let cool for a few minutes while you prepare the filling.

In a mixing bowl with an electric mixer, beat the cream cheese and granulated sugar, until creamy. Add the egg, lemon juice and vanilla and continue beating for another couple of minutes—until the mixture is smooth. Pour into the pre-baked crust and sprinkle evenly with the reserved crumbs (remember them?). Bake for 25 to 30 minutes—until just set but not yet browned.

Let cool in pan, then cut into squares.

Makes 25 squares. Just enough.

Clueless Troubleshooting: Cookies and Squares

Did your good cookies turn out bad? It's a devastating experience. We know. We feel your pain. We want to help.

The cookies spread out *too* much on the baking sheet.

- There may have been too much shortening (fat) in the dough. Increase the flour next time or reduce the shortening.
- The oven may not have been hot enough, causing the dough to splodge out before it set. Increase the temperature slightly and see what happens. (Check your oven temperature with a thermometer to see if it's accurate.)
- Was the cookie sheet warm from a previous batch? This can cause the dough to melt and spread before it actually begins baking. Cool the cookie sheet between batches (or use two sheets and alternate them).

The cookies were burnt on the bottom.

- Is your oven temperature accurate? Check it with an oven thermometer.
- If the pan was on the bottom shelf, move it up to the middle or upper shelf in the oven. If you were baking two pans at once, switch them around halfway through the baking time so that they bake more evenly.
- Dark baking sheets will brown the bottom of the cookies more quickly than shiny ones. Use shiny baking sheets, if possible, or line your baking sheets with foil.

Drat. The ¶&$˙#%! cookies stuck to the pan.

- Did you grease it? Really now—did you?
- Next time, line your baking sheets with parchment paper. You'll never have another stuck cookie. Guaranteed. And you don't have to replace the paper for each batch of cookies—just remove the baked ones, wipe the paper with a paper towel and keep right on baking.

The cookies were too hard when they cooled.

- They were overbaked. Cut down on baking time by a couple of minutes next time.
- Maybe there was too much flour in the dough. Reduce flour by a small amount and see if that helps.
- Put them in a container with a tight-fitting lid and throw in a chunk of apple. Let them fester together overnight and see what happens. Just might help.

The dough cracks when I try to roll it out.

- Too much flour. Reduce the amount of flour next time.
- Was the dough too cold? Let it warm up slightly (or knead it in your hands to soften it) before trying to roll it out.
- Add a teensy bit more liquid to the dough to make it more pliable.

The cookie dough is too sticky.

- Add a bit more flour to make it workable, and roll it out on a very well-floured surface. Dust your rolling pin with flour too.
- Chill the dough for an hour or two before rolling. Then, cut the dough into pieces and just roll a manageable portion of the dough at a time.

I wanted chewy brownies. These are crunchy.

- Always underbake brownies. When you think they just might be done—they are. They'll continue to solidify as they cool, so if they're a little too soft when you take them out of the oven, they'll be just right.

Cakes and Frostings

It's your birthday? You need a cake. You passed your eye exam? You need a cake. You got a new dog? It's cake time! A new friend? A parking ticket? A promotion? Athlete's foot? An inheritance? If you're happy, bake a cake to celebrate. If you're depressed, a cake will cheer you up. No matter how weird or wonderful the occasion, a cake is just the thing you need. You don't have an occasion? Invent one.

Cakes

Good Old Chocolate Cake

Who needs a cake mix? Surely not you.

Bigger takes longer

For complex scientific reasons, when you bake cake batter in one large pan (let's say, 9 x 13-inches/23 x 33 cm), the baking time will be slightly longer than for the same amount of batter in two smaller pans. The range of baking time indicated in the cake recipes cleverly takes this into account. Big pan, longer time. Small pan, shorter time. That's all there is to it.

2 cups	500 mL	all-purpose flour
2 cups	500 mL	granulated sugar
½ cup	125 mL	unsweetened cocoa powder
1 tsp	5 mL	baking powder
1 tsp	5 mL	baking soda
1 ½ cups	375 mL	milk
½ cup	125 mL	vegetable oil
1 tsp	5 mL	vanilla
2		eggs

Preheat the oven to 350° F (180° C). Prepare two greased and parchment-lined 9-inch (23 cm) round cake pans, *or* one 9 x 13-inch (23 x 33 cm) rectangular pan (see page 125). Set aside.

In a large mixing bowl, combine the flour, sugar, cocoa powder, baking powder and baking soda. Add the milk, vegetable oil and vanilla and beat with an electric mixer for about 2 minutes until smooth, scraping down the sides several times. Add the eggs and beat for another 2 minutes.

Pour batter into the prepared pans, then slam the pans on the counter once or twice to eliminate bubbles. Bake for 35 to 45 minutes or until a toothpick poked into the middle of the cake comes out clean. Let cool in the pan for 5 minutes, then invert onto a rack, peel off the paper, and let cool completely before doing something delicious with it.

Makes two 9-inch (23 cm) round layers or one 9 x 13-inch (23 x 33 cm) rectangular cake.

Preparing a Cake Pan

This is, frankly, not that much fun. Do it first—before you begin mixing the batter or dough—so you won't be tempted to skimp on this crucial task.

Cut a sheet of waxed paper or baker's parchment (see page 81) a little larger than your baking pan. Lay it on the counter, place the baking pan on top and, using a pencil, trace around the bottom of the pan. Using scissors, cut along the lines—you now have a paper liner that will fit exactly into the bottom of your pan.

Next, using vegetable shortening or non-stick baking spray, lightly grease the bottom and sides of your baking pan. Place the paper liner into the bottom of the pan, smoothing it out so that there are no wrinkles. Grease this paper liner and the sides of the pan again, and you are now ready to bake.

See? Aren't you happy that's over with?

Preparing a Cake Pan—An Advanced Technique

A recipe may tell you to "grease and flour" your pan. This is sometimes done with delicate cakes that are particularly prone to sticking. Here's what you do: prepare your cake pan as usual (line the bottom with paper) and grease the bottom and sides really well. Now sprinkle in a small amount (1 tbsp/15 mL) of flour and tilt the pan around, tapping it so that the flour sticks evenly to all the inside surfaces of the pan. Dump out any excess flour, pour in the batter and bake as usual. If you're making a chocolate cake, you can use cocoa powder instead of flour so that it doesn't show.

Divine Yellow Cake

Any cake can be cupcake

Almost any basic cake batter can be used to make cupcakes. Just spoon the cake batter into a paper-lined muffin pan, filling the cups about half full. Bake for half the time necessary to bake a full-sized cake, then test with a toothpick to see if it's done (see page 28). If not, continue baking for another 5 minutes or so, until it's ready. Slather with icing (of course) when completely cooled.

Ridiculously easy, light and delicious—this cake can handle whatever you care to throw at it, especially strawberries and whipped cream.

2 cups	500 mL	granulated sugar
4		eggs
¾ cup	175 mL	vegetable oil
1 cup	250 mL	milk
2 ½ cups	625 mL	all-purpose flour
2 ¼ tsp	11 mL	baking powder
1 tsp	5 mL	vanilla

Preheat the oven to 350° F (180° C). Prepare two greased and parchment-lined 9-inch (23 cm) round cake pans, *or* one 9 x 13-inch (23 x 33 cm) rectangular pan (see page 125). Set aside.

In a large mixing bowl, with an electric mixer, beat the sugar and eggs together until slightly thickened—about 1 minute. Add the oil, milk, flour, baking powder and vanilla, and beat for another minute—just until the batter is smooth and creamy. Don't overbeat it.

Pour batter into the prepared baking pans. Bake for 30 to 40 minutes, until the tops are golden and a toothpick poked into the center of the layer comes out clean.

Run a knife around the sides of the cake to loosen it from the pan, then turn the layers out onto a rack to cool completely before having your way with them.

Makes two 9-inch (22 cm) round layers, or one 9 x 13-inch (23 x 33 cm) rectangular cake.

Classic Carrot Cake

Why would any sane person put carrots in a cake? Was it an accident? A misprinted recipe? A joke? Does it really matter? It's a classic.

2 cups	500 mL	all-purpose flour
2 tsp	10 mL	baking powder
1 ½ tsp	7 mL	baking soda
1 tsp	5 mL	cinnamon
2 cups	500 mL	granulated sugar
1 cup	250 mL	vegetable oil
4		eggs
2 cups	500 mL	grated carrots (about 3 medium carrots)
1 cup	250 mL	canned crushed pineapple, well drained
½ cup	125 mL	chopped pecans

Preheat the oven to 350° F (180° C). Prepare two greased and parchment-lined 8 or 9-inch (20 or 23 cm) round cake pans, *or* one 9 x 13-inch (23 x 33 cm) rectangular pan. Set aside.

In a medium bowl, stir together the flour, baking powder, baking soda and cinnamon.

In a large bowl, with an electric mixer, beat together the sugar, oil and eggs until smooth. Add the flour mixture to the egg mixture, stir, then mix in the carrots, pineapple and pecans. Pour this batter into the prepared baking pans. Bake for 40 to 50 minutes or until a toothpick poked into the middle comes out clean.

Remove cake from the pan, peel off the paper, and let cool thoroughly on a rack before frosting with (what else?) Cream Cheese Frosting (see page 165).

Makes one 8 or 9-inch (20 or 23 cm) round cake or one 9 x 13-inch (23 x 33 cm) rectangular cake.

Sponge Roll Cake

Extremely impressive. Easier than anything.

Cake

¾ cup	175 mL	all-purpose flour
¾ tsp	3 mL	baking powder
4		eggs
¾ cup	175 mL	granulated sugar
1 tsp	5 mL	vanilla
		icing sugar for dusting

Filling

1 cup	250 mL	jam or jelly, any kind, *or*
2 cups	500 mL	sweetened whipped cream (see page 150), *or*
2 cups	500 mL	Creamy Chocolate or Vanilla Frosting (see page 162 or 163)

Preheat the oven to 400° F (200° C). Prepare a jelly roll pan or cookie pan approximately 10 x 15 inches (25 x 38 cm), with ½-inch (1 cm) sides. Grease it lightly, then line the bottom with parchment paper or waxed paper, and grease the paper lightly as well. Set aside.

In a small bowl, mix together the flour and the baking powder. Set aside.

In a mixing bowl, beat the eggs with an electric mixer until foamy. Add the sugar and vanilla and continue beating until the mixture becomes very light and thick and has doubled in volume. This will take between 5 and 7 minutes. Now gently fold in the flour mixture (sprinkle it over the surface and stir it into the egg mixture using a rubber spatula), taking care not to deflate the batter. When the flour is thoroughly mixed in (don't overmix), spread the batter evenly in the prepared pan (carefully smooth out any bumps). Bake for 8 or 9 minutes until very lightly browned and the cake springs back when you touch it on top. Remove from the oven and let cool for 2 or 3 minutes in the pan.

Now...sprinkle a clean dish towel (no really—do it) with icing sugar. Loosen the cake from the sides of the pan and (quickly! carefully! watch out!!!) flip the cake out onto the sugared towel. Peel off the paper (ta da!). With a sharp knife, trim off the crispy edges (and eat them—this is the cook's bonus).

Now, fill it and roll it up. Choose one of the following options:

To fill with jam or jelly: Spread the jam or jelly onto the still-warm cake. Carefully roll up (starting with the long side) as tightly as possible without squishing it. You can use the towel to help roll the cake. Let cool completely, wrapped in the towel. Sprinkle with more icing sugar before serving (unwrapped!).

To fill with whipped cream or frosting: While the cake is still warm, gently roll it in the towel (starting with the long side) and let cool completely. You have to do this because you can't spread whipped cream or buttercream frosting on a warm cake, and once the cake has cooled, it will be impossible to roll it up without cracking. When the cake has completely cooled, carefully unroll it, spread it with whipped cream or creamy chocolate or vanilla frosting, and re-roll it, as firmly as possible without squishing. Sprinkle with more icing sugar before serving.

Chocolate variation

Reduce the flour in the recipe to ½ cup (125 mL), and sift together with ¼ cup (50 mL) unsweetened cocoa powder. Otherwise, prepare and fill as usual.

Angel Food Cake

Deceptively simple, this cake can be a bit temperamental to bake. But if you follow the recipe exactly and give it your undivided attention, you should end up with an almost inconceivably light cake. Almost a marshmallow.

1 cup	250 mL	cake and pastry flour, sifted
1 ½ cups	375 mL	granulated sugar, divided
1 ½ cups	375 mL	egg whites (about 12 eggs)
1 ½ tsp	7 mL	cream of tartar
1 ½ tsp	7 mL	vanilla

Preheat the oven to 375° F (190° C).

Sift the flour, measure it and sift it two more times with the ¾ cup (175 mL) of the sugar (please, *please* note—this is only *half* the total amount of sugar).

In a large mixing bowl with an electric mixer, beat the egg whites until just foamy. Add the cream of tartar and the vanilla and continue beating until they form soft peaks but are still moist and glossy. Now, *very gradually*, add the *remaining* ¾ cup (175 mL) of the sugar, a couple of spoonfuls at a time. Beat after each addition, scraping the sides of the bowl to make sure the sugar is thoroughly incorporated. Continue beating until all the sugar has been added and the egg whites form a stiff peak when you lift the beater out of the bowl.

Add the flour gradually, in 3 or 4 additions, by *sifting* it over the beaten egg whites, and folding it very gently into the mixture with a wide rubber scraper. Repeat until all the flour mixture has been added and the batter is smooth but not deflated. Pour into an *ungreased* 10-inch (25 cm) tube pan (the kind with a removable bottom).

Bake for 35 to 40 minutes or until it is light brown and the top springs back when you touch it. *Do not open the door midway through the baking time just to see how things are going.* Remember—this cake can be moody and irritable, so do not aggravate it.

Place a wine bottle (or other long-necked bottle) on the counter. Remove the cake from the oven and immediately invert the pan onto the neck of the bottle—sliding the tube part of the pan over the neck. This will allow the cake to firm up and cool without collapsing under its own weight. Don't worry—it won't fall out. Let it cool completely. When it has cooled, remove it from the bottle and turn it right side up. Carefully loosen the sides of the cake by running a knife around the edges and around the tube, then lift out the middle, loosen it from the bottom of the pan and invert onto a plate to serve.

Makes one ethereally light cake that is impossibly delicious with strawberries and whipped cream.

What's with the ungreased pan?

Leaving the baking pan *ungreased* when making an Angel Food Cake (or any other light and fluffy tube cake) allows the batter to grip the sides of the pan as it rises. This helps it to rise nice and high—which is what you want it to do. The batter is so fluffy and delicate that it needs a little help on the way up.

Don't we all?

Practically Perfect Pound Cake

Pound cake. So plain but so good. With ice cream or fruit. With chocolate sauce. It's even delicious straight from the freezer (yes, we know you've done that). Here's a basic pound cake recipe—with a few not-so-basic variations.

2 cups	500 mL	all-purpose flour
1 tsp	5 mL	baking powder
¾ cup	175 mL	unsalted butter
1 cup	250 mL	granulated sugar
3		eggs
2 tsp	10 mL	vanilla
½ cup	125 mL	milk

Preheat the oven to 325° F (160° C). Grease a 9 x 5-inch (23 x 13 cm) loaf pan. Set aside.

In a bowl, stir together the flour and the baking powder. Set aside.

In a large bowl with an electric mixer, beat together the butter and sugar until well mixed. Add the eggs, one at a time, beating well after each egg. Continue beating the mixture for 2 or 3 minutes after all the eggs have been added. Beat in the vanilla, then add the flour mixture, in 2 or 3 additions, alternately with the milk, beating until the batter is just smooth. Dump into the prepared loaf pan. Bake for 70 to 75 minutes, until a toothpick poked into the center of the cake comes out clean.

Let cool in the pan for 10 minutes, then remove and let cool completely on a rack before having your way with it.

Makes one practically perfect pound cake.

Variations

Chocolate Swirl Pound Cake

Melt 1 square (1 oz/28 g) semisweet chocolate with 2 tbsp (30 mL) milk in a small saucepan over low heat. Stir until smooth. Divide the plain batter equally into two bowls and beat the chocolate mixture into one half. Spoon the two batters—the chocolate and the plain—alternately into the greased loaf pan, then run a knife or narrow spatula through the batter to swirl them together gently. Bake as if it were normal.

Lemon or Orange Pound Cake

Omit the vanilla from the basic recipe. Add the grated zest from one lemon or one orange and 1 tbsp (15 mL) lemon or orange juice to the batter when you add the flour and the milk. Bake as above.

Poppy Seed Pound Cake

Add 2 tbsp (30 mL) poppy seeds to either plain or lemon pound cake batter when you add the flour. Bake as above.

Vanilla

Shy but talented, poor quiet vanilla rarely gets the respect it deserves. I mean, vanilla ice cream is even white, for heaven's sake. Like it doesn't even have a color. No wonder it's not taken seriously.

The vanilla bean itself is the seed pod of an orchid. This whole pod is slowly dried, turning it dark brown and developing the characteristic vanilla flavor. Sometimes you can find these whole vanilla beans sold in specialty stores. These can be used to flavor sugar or cooked desserts. But vanilla is most often sold as "extract"—basically alcohol that has been infused with the flavor of the vanilla bean. It's expensive. But worth it.

Artificial or imitation vanilla extract is much cheaper and is sold in great big bottles. You think you're getting a bargain. You're not. It tastes chemical and fake. Go for the real thing. If you're already baking from scratch, you don't want to use junky ingredients do you?

Accidental Trifle

You didn't mean to drop half the cake on the floor. Now what do you do with it? Well, pick up the pieces, fish out the bits of dirt and dog hair and make this lovely trifle.

1		stale or otherwise ruined layer cake or pound cake, any kind
6 cups	1.5 liters	strawberries, raspberries, blueberries, peaches, bananas (or any combination thereof)
¼ cup	50 mL	granulated sugar
1 recipe		prepared cream filling from vanilla cream pie (see page 188) or (if you must cheat) 1 prepared vanilla pudding, prepared
2 cups	500 mL	35% (whipping) cream
2 tbsp	30 mL	granulated sugar
¼ cup	50 mL	sherry (any kind)
1 cup	250 mL	raspberry or apricot jam

Cut the cake up into slices, as evenly as you can—they can be ragged or funny shaped; it doesn't matter. Prepare the fruit (wash, slice, peel, do whatever must be done) and toss it with ¼ cup (50 mL) of the sugar. Prepare the cream filling and let it cool (or make up a batch of vanilla pudding, you cheater).

Pour the whipping cream into a large bowl and add the remaining 2 tbsp (30 mL) of sugar. Beat with an electric mixer on high speed until the cream is thick and holds a soft peak when you lift the beaters from the bowl (eek—turn them off first!). Set aside.

OK, arrange about half of the cake slices in a layer on the bottom of your prettiest glass bowl (approximately 8-inch/20 cm diameter). Sprinkle the cake slices with half of the sherry, then spread with half of the jam. Top with half of the fruit, then slather with half of the cream filled. Cover with half of the whipped cream.

Now repeat: the rest of the cake slices, more sherry, the rest of the jam, the rest of the fruit, the rest of the custard and the rest of the whipped cream. Smooth the top of the whipped cream and decorate with a few extra berries or whatever you happen to have hanging around.

There you go. No one will ever suspect the deep dark truth. You *know* what I mean.

Makes 8 to 10 servings.

Note

This trifle can also be made with perfectly sound, non-stale pound or yellow cake. In fact, we'd recommend it.

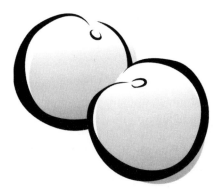

European Hazelnut Torte

Let's say your cousin Zsa Zsa from Budapest is coming for dinner.
This is what she would expect for dessert. Nothing less. Lucky for you,
it's easy.

Cake

4		eggs
¾ cup	175 mL	granulated sugar
1 cup	250 mL	whole hazelnuts
2 tbsp	30 mL	all-purpose flour
2 ½ tsp	12 mL	baking powder
¼ cup	50 mL	apricot jam

Coffee Whipped Cream

1 ½ cups	375 mL	35% (whipping) cream
½ cup	125 mL	granulated sugar
2 tbsp	30 mL	instant coffee powder
2 tsp	10 mL	vanilla

Preheat the oven to 350° F (180° C). Grease two 8-inch (20 cm) round cake pans and line them with parchment. Set aside.

In a blender (preferably) or a food processor, combine the eggs and sugar and blend at high speed until smooth and creamy. Now add the hazelnuts—yes, whole. Put the lid back on the container and blend until the nuts are finely ground, scraping down the sides of the container with a rubber scraper once or twice. Now add the flour and the baking powder and blend just until combined.

Pour the batter into the prepared cake pans. Bake for 15 to 20 minutes or until very lightly browned. If they're done, the cakes will spring back when you touch the top lightly.

Let the layers cool for about 5 minutes, then loosen the sides of the cake from the pans by running a knife around the edges, and invert them onto a rack. Peel off the paper and let the layers cool completely. Completely.

Prepare the Coffee Whipped Cream. Combine the whipping cream, sugar, instant coffee powder, and vanilla in a large bowl and beat with an electric mixer until the cream is thick and forms stiff peaks. Don't overbeat the mixture because you will end up with coffee-flavored butter instead of whipped cream. If you're not sure, then just stop.

When you are ready to assemble the cake, place one layer on a serving plate and spread with apricot jam. Place the second cake layer over it. Cover the top and sides evenly with the coffee whipped cream and garnish tastefully in a sophisticated, European manner. That means no plastic spacemen.

Well, OK, just one spaceman. But no Pokemon figures.

Makes one perfect 8-inch (20 cm) torte.

Smashed Caramel Garnish

You won't believe how cool this looks on a cake.

Measure 1 cup (250 mL) granulated sugar into a small, heavy-bottomed saucepan. Place over low heat and cook, without stirring, until the sugar begins to melt and caramelize. Continue to cook, stirring once in a while, until it is completely melted and golden. Remove from heat (immediately—you don't want it to burn) and pour onto a greased baking sheet, spreading it into a thin layer. Let cool until completely hard, about 10 minutes.

Pry the sheet of hardened sugar off the baking sheet, and crack it into uneven shards. Make some big ones, some smaller ones, some pointy ones. Arrange these pieces, standing up randomly, in the icing on your cake. Anything too small to use as a decoration can be eaten by you. You deserve it.

There. Smashing, isn't it?

Lethal Chocolate Cupcakes

The chocolate cupcake. Simple. Innocent. Harmless. Right? Wrong. You've been warned.

1 ½ cups	375 mL	all-purpose flour
¾ cup	175 mL	granulated sugar
¼ cup	50 mL	unsweetened cocoa powder
1 tsp	5 mL	baking soda
1 cup	250 mL	milk
¼ cup	50 mL	vegetable oil
1 tbsp	15 mL	white vinegar
1 tsp	5 mL	vanilla

Preheat the oven to 375° F (190° C). Grease a 12-cup muffin pan or line the cups with paper liners. Set aside.

In a medium bowl, stir together the flour, sugar, cocoa powder and baking soda. Add milk, oil, vinegar and vanilla. Beat with a whisk or electric mixer just until smooth.

Spoon batter into the prepared muffin pan, filling the cups about ¾ full. Bake for 15 to 20 minutes until a toothpick inserted into the center of a cupcake comes out clean. Remove cupcakes from pan and let cool on a rack.

Oh, sure you can eat them just like this. But why stop there? Dip each cooled cupcake into a bowl of Chocolate Ganache Glaze (see page 166) just to give the tops a shiny chocolate coating. Let cool until the glaze is set.

Makes 12 perfectly lethal cupcakes.

More Chocolate Silliness

Drizzle it!

Melt semisweet chocolate in the usual way (see page 93) and pour it into a small plastic sandwich bag. Cut off one corner (a very small snip, please) and drizzle melted chocolate over cookies, cakes or wherever you feel chocolate is necessary (it's none of our business). When you're done drizzling, simply throw the bag away and get on with life.

Squiggle it!

Make weird and wonderful chocolate cake decorations by drizzling crazy patterns and squiggles onto waxed paper and letting them harden. Peel off and use them to festoon a cake or pie.

Scribble it!

Write the birthday person's name in chocolate on waxed paper. Refrigerate until hard, then peel off the paper and use it to personalize a birthday cake. She'll be so impressed. (Special note: It is illegal to write rude things in chocolate. It just is.)

Shatter it!

Pour melted chocolate onto a waxed paper–lined cookie sheet, spreading it out into a thin sheet. Refrigerate until hard, then peel off the paper and break the chocolate into big irregular shards. Use these to decorate a cake or pie in an extremely artistic (yet slightly menacing) manner. Very cool.

Curl it!

Hold a square of chocolate in your hand until it's slightly warm. Using a vegetable peeler, shave off thin slices of chocolate—they'll fall off in tubular curls. Don't handle the curls because they'll melt in your hand. Use a spoon to transfer them to wherever you're putting them.

Anything Upside-Down Cake

For once, upside down is not an accident. Really—we meant to do that.

2 cups	500 mL	apples, pears or peaches, peeled and thinly sliced
2 tbsp	30 mL	butter, melted
½ cup	125 mL	light brown sugar
1 tbsp	15 mL	lemon juice
1 cup	250 mL	granulated sugar
2		eggs
⅓ cup	75 mL	vegetable oil
½ cup	125 mL	milk
1 ¼ cups	300 mL	all-purpose flour
1 tsp	5 mL	baking powder
1 tsp	5 mL	vanilla

Preheat the oven to 350° F (180° C).

In an 8-inch (20 cm) square baking pan or a 9-inch (23 cm) round baking pan, mix together the sliced fruit with the melted butter, the brown sugar and the lemon juice. Stir until everything is evenly coated, then arrange the slices on the bottom of the pan in an artistic and decorative manner. Or just carelessly spread them out in a single layer. Whatever.

In a bowl with an electric mixer, beat the granulated sugar and the eggs together until slightly thickened—about 1 minute. Add the oil, milk, flour, baking powder and vanilla and beat for another minute— just until the batter is smooth and creamy. Pour the batter over the fruit in the baking pan and bake for 30 to 35 minutes until very lightly browned.

When it's finished baking, remove cake from the oven. Let the upside-down cake (which is still right side up at this point) cool for 5 minutes, then run a knife around the edges of the pan to loosen it. Hold a plate over the pan and, all at once, flip the thing over. The upside-down cake should now be properly upside down, and the artistically arranged fruit should be clearly visible. If any fruit slices remain clinging to the baking pan, just scrape them off and rearrange them on the cake. Serve warm with ice cream. Or plain.

Makes 6 to 8 servings.

Chocolate Chip Banana Cake

Here's the perfect afterlife for those squishy black bananas you forgot about. And who says there's no such thing as reincarnation?

3		large, ripe bananas
1 cup	250 mL	light brown sugar
1/3 cup	75 mL	vegetable oil
1		egg
1 tsp	5 mL	vanilla
1 3/4 cups	425 mL	all-purpose flour
1 1/2 tsp	7 mL	baking powder
1 cup	250 mL	semisweet chocolate chips

Preheat the oven to 350° F (180° C). Grease an 8-inch (20 cm) square baking pan. Set aside.

In the container of a blender or food processor, combine the bananas, brown sugar, vegetable oil, egg and vanilla. Blend until smooth, scraping down the sides of the container once or twice.

In a large bowl, stir together the flour and the baking powder. Add the blended banana mixture to the bowl, stirring until everything is evenly combined. Stir in the chocolate chips. Spread batter in the prepared baking pan and bake for 30 to 35 minutes or until a toothpick poked into the middle of the cake comes out clean.

Let cool before frosting with (may I recommend?) Fudgy Sour Cream Frosting (see page 165) or Chocolate Ganache Glaze (see page 166).

Makes one 8-inch (20 cm) square cake.

Flourless Chocolate Cake

How can it be? A cake with no flour? What holds it together?
Puh-leeease—one must never question perfection.

2 cups	500 mL	semisweet chocolate chips
¾ cup	175 mL	unsalted butter
6 tbsp	90 mL	unsweetened cocoa powder
10		eggs, separated
⅔ cup	150 mL	granulated sugar
		icing sugar, sweetened whipped cream
		and fresh berries for garnish

Preheat the oven to 350° F (180° C).

Prepare a 10-inch (25 cm) springform pan for action. Using the bottom of the pan as a template, trace a circle onto baker's parchment paper (or waxed paper), then cut it out. Lightly grease the bottom of the pan, line with the circle of paper, then thoroughly grease the bottom and sides of the pan. Set aside.

In a saucepan over boiling water, melt the chocolate chips and butter together, stirring until smooth. Add the cocoa powder and stir to blend completely. Set aside.

In a very large, *scrupulously* clean mixing bowl beat the egg whites, with an electric mixer at high speed, until foamy. Gradually add the sugar—a spoonful at a time—continuing to beat until stiff and glossy. Set this aside too.

In another large bowl, beat the egg yolks for 5 minutes—until they just begin to thicken. Add the melted chocolate mixture, and beat until very well combined. Stir in about ¼ of the egg whites to lighten the mixture, then *very gently* fold in the remaining egg whites until fairly well combined. Don't overmix the batter in an effort to eliminate all the streaks of white—better a few streaks than deflated batter. Pour into the prepared baking pan, then bake for 40 to 45 minutes. The center of the cake will still be a bit soft. Fine.

Remove the pan from the oven and let it cool for about 10 minutes. Loosen the sides of the cake by running a sharp knife around the edges, then invert the cake onto a plate. Peel off the paper and let the cake cool completely at room temperature. Refrigerate, covered loosely with plastic wrap, if you're not planning to serve it within a couple of hours.

Just before serving, remove from refrigerator, and dust the top of cake with icing sugar. Garnish each slice of cake with a glop of whipped cream and some fresh berries, if you have them. Be prepared to swoon.

Makes one 10-inch (25 cm) cake, approximately 12 intensely chocolate servings.

Chocolate Leaves—The Ultimate Cake Decoration

Remember those horrible icing flowers on bakery cakes you used to love so much? Or maybe you still do. Well, here's something better—chocolate leaves. Not only do they look gorgeous, but, well, they're chocolate. And easy to do. Guaranteed to make you famous.

You'll need

- Semisweet chocolate (squares or bars, *not chips*)

- Sturdy, non-poisonous leaves—like rose or lemon leaves (make sure they haven't been sprayed with chemicals)

- Waxed paper

First, line a baking sheet or tray with a sheet of waxed paper. Wash the leaves and make sure they're perfectly dry.

Now melt a few squares of semisweet chocolate (see chocolate melting instructions on page 93) stirring until smooth. Using a thin spatula or flat brush, spread a layer of chocolate onto the underside of the leaves, almost (but not quite) all the way to the edges. Place the leaves, chocolate side up, onto the waxed paper–lined tray. Refrigerate for 10 minutes until the chocolate has hardened. Working quickly, peel the leaf away from the chocolate, giving you a realistic, edible chocolate leaf, which you can use to festoon your next cake. Keep refrigerated until you use them and handle them as little as possible—the warmth of your hand will melt them.

There. Now isn't that impressive?

Pure Cheesecake

Don't forget to floss!

Your cake, that is.

Dental floss is the best thing to use to slice cheesecake. Really.

Just cut a length of floss wider than the diameter of your cake, hold one end in each hand, and press downward as if you were using a knife. It will give you perfect, straight slices with no gooey bits messing up the edges. Gorgeous.

Everyone needs a good cheesecake recipe. This one is rich, without being heavy, and lends itself to all sorts of excellent variations. Make it once, and you're set for life, cheesecakewise.

Crumb Crust

1 ½ cups	375 mL	graham cracker or chocolate wafer crumbs
2 tbsp	30 mL	granulated sugar
¼ cup	50 mL	butter, melted

Filling

1 ½ lbs	750 g	cream cheese, softened (three 8 oz/250 g packages)
4		large eggs
2 tsp	10 mL	vanilla
1 cup	250 mL	granulated sugar

Preheat the oven to 350° F (180° C).

Make the crust by stirring together the crumbs with the sugar and butter. Dump into a 10-inch (25 cm) greased springform pan and press firmly onto the bottom (*not* up the sides) of the pan. Bake for 10 minutes. Let cool while you prepare the filling.

In a large bowl with an electric mixer, beat the cream cheese until fluffy. Add the eggs, one at a time, beating well after each one. Beat in the vanilla and the sugar, then pour into the pre-baked crumb crust. Slam the pan down onto the counter a couple of times to eliminate any bubbles.

Bake for 45 to 50 minutes—the cake will still be quite moist in the middle, a little wobbly even. That's fine—it will set as it cools. Remove from the oven and let cool completely.

When the cake is completely cool, the top may be uneven, with the sides being higher than the middle. Since you will probably cover the cake with a glaze or fruit topping, this is not a problem. So just ignore it. (You can also serve it plain, if you like. There's no law against that.)

Spread the topping (see page 146) evenly over the surface of the cake, or leave it plain if you prefer. Chill the cheesecake for several hours or overnight before removing the sides of the pan.

Makes one 10-inch (25 cm) cheesecake—at least 12 servings.

Variations on a Cheesecake

Chocolate Swirl Cheesecake

Melt 2 squares (1 oz/28 g each) semisweet chocolate (see page 93). Remove 2 cups (500 mL) of the prepared cheesecake filling mixture to a bowl and beat in the melted chocolate, mixing until blended. Spoon the chocolate mixture into the plain mixture and swirl it together, very gently, with a spatula or a wide-bladed knife. (Better to leave it a little less mixed than to overblend it and lose the swirls.) Turn this mixture into the pan, but try not to wreck the nice marbled effect. Bake as above.

Raspberry Swirl Cheesecake

Into the prepared cheesecake filling mixture, spoon 1 cup (250 mL) canned raspberry pie filling (or homemade raspberry puree, cooked with cornstarch to thicken) in large dollops. Swirl the raspberry goop through the plain cheesecake mixture very gently with a wide-bladed knife or spatula. You want to create ripples of raspberry through the cake, so don't overmix it. Turn this mixture into the crust-lined pan, being careful not to mess up the swirls. Bake as above.

Irish Cream Cheesecake

This is easy. Omit the vanilla from the plain cheesecake recipe and, instead, add ⅓ cup (75 mL) Irish cream liqueur. Bake as above.

Over-the-Top Toppings

Chocolate Glaze

Melt together 6 squares (1 oz/28 g each) semisweet chocolate and ½ cup (125 mL) whipping cream over low heat. Stir until smooth and pour evenly over the surface of the baked and cooled cheesecake, spreading to cover the top evenly—then leave it alone to chill in peace.

Fruit Topping

Spread 1 cup (250 mL) canned raspberry, strawberry, blueberry or peach pie filling over the baked and cooled cheesecake. Chill.

Fresh Berry Topping

Arrange whole fresh berries (any kind—whatever is in season) over the entire surface of the baked and cooled cheesecake. Heat 1 cup (250 mL) strawberry or apple jelly just until liquidy and spoon over the berries to glaze them. Chill until the glaze sets.

Sour Cream Topping

Stir together 1 cup (250 mL) sour cream, 2 tbsp (30 mL) sugar and 1 tsp (5 mL) vanilla in a small bowl. Spread over top of cheesecake as soon as it comes out of the oven, then return it to the oven and bake for an additional 10 minutes. Cool and chill.

The Clueless Baker

Marble Bundt Cake

Here's a nice, substantial marble cake that can hold its own with a cup of espresso or a tall glass of cold milk. It needs nothing more than a dusting of icing sugar to finish it off.

¾ cup	175 mL	butter, softened
1 ½ cups	375 mL	granulated sugar + ½ Brown
3 +1 yolk		eggs
1 ½ tsp	7 mL	vanilla
¾ cup	175 mL	milk
2 ½ cups	675 mL	all-purpose flour
2 tsp	10 mL	baking powder
½ cup	125 mL	chocolate syrup (the regular chocolate milk kind)
¼ tsp	1 mL	baking soda
		icing sugar for dusting

Preheat the oven to 325° F (160° C). Grease a large (12-cup/3 liter) bundt pan. Set aside.

In a large bowl, with an electric mixer, beat together the butter, sugar, eggs and vanilla, until very smooth and creamy—about 2 or 3 minutes. While you continue beating, add the milk, a little at a time. Beat for another minute or so, until the mixture is smooth.

In another bowl, stir together the flour and baking powder. Add this to the butter mixture—in 3 or 4 portions—and beat just until everything is combined.

Now, pour about ⅔ of the batter into the prepared bundt pan. To the remaining batter, add the chocolate syrup and the baking soda and beat with an electric mixer just until blended. Spoon the chocolate batter into the pan over the white batter then, using a spatula or knife, gently swirl the two batters together—don't blend them into a muck—you want to retain the marbled effect.

Bake for 1 to 1 ¼ hours or until a toothpick poked into the thickest part of the cake comes out clean. Allow the cake to cool in the pan for about half an hour, then loosen the sides gently with a knife and invert the cake onto a plate or cooling rack. Sprinkle heavily with icing sugar just before serving.

Makes one nice big cake.

Poppy Seed Yogurt Bundt Cake

Light, delicious, filled with enough poppy seeds to leave you picking your teeth for hours afterward.

1 cup	250 mL	plain yogurt
½ cup	125 mL	poppy seeds
1 cup	250 mL	granulated sugar
¾ cup	175 mL	vegetable oil
4		eggs
2 tsp	10 mL	vanilla
2 ½ cups	625 mL	all-purpose flour
2 tsp	10 mL	baking powder
1 tsp	5 mL	baking soda

In a small bowl, stir together the yogurt and the poppy seeds and let soak while you gather ingredients and prepare the rest of the recipe.

Preheat the oven to 325° F (160° C). Grease a 10-inch (25 cm) bundt pan.

In a large mixing bowl, with an electric mixer, beat together the sugar, vegetable oil, eggs and vanilla for 2 or 3 minutes, until thickened.

In another bowl, stir together the flour, baking powder and baking soda. Add the flour mixture to the egg mixture, in 2 or 3 additions, alternately with the poppy seed mixture. Beat just until smooth. Pour into the prepared bundt pan and bake for 50 to 60 minutes, until it passes the toothpick test (see page 28). Remove from oven and let cool for 10 minutes before removing it from the pan. Let cool completely on a rack.

Drizzle cooled cake with Shiny Sugar Glaze (see page 167—the lemon version is especially recommended), dust with icing sugar or just leave it naked.

Makes one 10-inch (25 cm) bundt cake (about 12 servings).

Chocolate Lava Cakes

These seemingly harmless (ha!) little chocolate cakes erupt with molten chocolate lava when you poke a fork into them. Abandon all hope—there's no escape.

5 squares		**(1 oz/28 g each) semisweet chocolate**
¼ cup	**50 mL**	**butter**
1 tbsp	**15 mL**	**brandy or other liqueur**
2		**eggs**
2		**additional egg yolks**
¼ cup	**50 mL**	**granulated sugar**
1 tsp	**5 mL**	**vanilla**
1 tsp	**5 mL**	**instant coffee powder**
1 tbsp	**15 mL**	**all-purpose flour**
		whipped cream as an accompaniment

Grease four ¾-cup (175 mL) custard cups or souffle dishes. Set aside.

In a small saucepan, combine the chocolate and butter and place over low heat. Cook, stirring, until the chocolate is melted and the mixture is smooth. Remove from heat and stir in the brandy. Let cool for a few minutes.

Meanwhile, in a medium bowl, with an electric mixer, beat together the eggs, additional egg yolks, sugar, vanilla and instant coffee powder until very thick, about 5 minutes. The mixture should form a gloopy ribbon when you lift the beater from the bowl. Fold in the flour and the chocolate mixture, mixing just until combined.

Pour batter into the prepared custard cups or souffle dishes. Cover with plastic wrap and refrigerate until about 45 minutes before you're ready to serve dessert. (In fact, you can do this up to a whole day ahead of time. Really!)

Remove from the refrigerator and let stand at room temperature for 30 minutes before baking.

Preheat the oven to 400° F (200° C).

Place custard cups on a baking sheet and bake for 15 minutes, until a toothpick poked into the center of one of the cups comes out with moist batter still attached. (These should be *drastically underbaked* in order to produce the crucial lava effect.) Let cool for 5 minutes, then carefully loosen the sides and turn them out onto individual serving plates.

Whipped cream is mandatory. Chocolate shavings are optional.

Makes 4 thoroughly evil servings.

Whipped Cream—It's Always a Good Thing.

Whipped cream is never out of place. You can plop a blob on something as mundane as a brownie, or swirl it on top of a creamy cheesecake. Here are some possibilities.

Plain Sweetened Whipped Cream

1 cup	250 mL	whipping cream
2 tbsp	30 mL	granulated sugar

First of all, make sure everything you'll be using—the bowl, the beaters and the cream—are very cold. It's helpful (but not absolutely necessary) to stash the bowl and beaters in the freezer for a few minutes before beating. Warmth is the enemy of whipped cream.

Pour the whipping cream into the cold mixing bowl and add the sugar. Beat with an electric mixer on high speed, scraping down the sides of the bowl from time to time, until thickened. Stop beating as soon as the cream is thick enough to mound up when you drop it from a spoon. Beating it beyond that point may cause it to curdle horribly and turn, eventually, into butter.

There you are. Use it in any way you see fit.

Makes about 2 cups (500 mL) whipped cream.

Chocolate Whipped Cream

Increase sugar to ¼ cup (50 mL) and add 2 tbsp (30 mL) unsweetened cocoa powder to the basic mixture before whipping.

Mocha Whipped Cream

Increase sugar to ¼ cup (50 mL) and add 2 tbsp (30 mL) unsweetened cocoa powder and 1 tsp (5 mL) instant coffee powder to the basic mixture before whipping.

Strawberry (or Raspberry) Whipped Cream

Increase the sugar to ¼ cup (50 mL), then whip. Fold ½ cup (125 mL) unsweetened pureed strawberries or raspberries (frozen ones are just fine, but of course, fresh ones are even finer) into the whipped cream and beat briefly until combined.

Horrible Holiday Fruitcake

Even if you don't actually like fruitcake, you'll probably like this one. Light and fruity (not dark and heavy), it's definitely not the usual doorstop.

2 cups	500 mL	all-purpose flour
1 tsp	5 mL	baking powder
2 cups	500 mL	coarsely chopped pecans or walnuts
½ cup	125 mL	golden raisins
¼ cup	50 mL	candied pineapple, chopped
¼ cup	50 mL	red candied cherries, chopped
¼ cup	50 mL	green candied cherries, chopped
1 cup	250 mL	butter
1 ¼ cups	300 mL	granulated sugar
3		eggs
2 tbsp	30 mL	orange juice or brandy
2 tsp	10 mL	grated lemon zest
2 tsp	10 mL	vanilla
		brandy or liqueur for brushing

Preheat the oven to 300° F (150° C). Grease two small—3 ½ x 7 ½ inch (9 x 19 cm)—loaf pans (disposable aluminum ones are the perfect size). Set aside.

In a bowl, stir together the flour and the baking powder until evenly mixed.

In another bowl, mix together the pecans, raisins, pineapple and cherries. Remove 2 tbsp (30 mL) of the flour mixture from the bowl and toss with the fruit until everything is evenly coated. Set both the fruit mixture and the flour mixture aside.

Now in a very large mixing bowl, with an electric mixer, cream together the butter and sugar until light and fluffy—this will take about 5 minutes or so. Add the eggs, one at a time, beating well after each one. Then beat in the flour mixture, in two or three portions, alternately with the orange juice or brandy.

Finally stir in the fruit mixture, lemon zest and vanilla, mixing just until everything is evenly combined. Spoon batter into the prepared loaf pans. Bake for about 2 hours—until a toothpick poked into the center of a cake comes out clean.

Let cakes cool for 30 minutes in the pans, then remove and let cool completely. Brush the top and sides generously with brandy (or whatever liqueur you like), wrap tightly in foil and let them fester for at least a couple of days before serving.

Makes two horrible fruitcakes—one for you and one to give to someone you, um, love.

Chocolate Chip Zucchini Cake

If you're drowning in a bumper crop of zucchini, this cake won't put much of a dent in the oversupply. But even so, it's worth making. In fact, it's worth making even if you have to go out and buy a zuke!

1 cup	250 mL	granulated sugar
¼ cup	50 mL	vegetable oil
2		eggs
1 tsp	5 mL	vanilla
1 ¼ cups	300 mL	all-purpose flour
2 tsp	10 mL	baking powder
½ tsp	2 mL	cinnamon
1 cup	250 mL	shredded zucchini (one 6-inch/ 15 cm zuke)
½ cup	125 mL	semi-sweet chocolate chips

Preheat the oven to 375° F (190° C). Grease an 8-inch (20 cm) square baking pan. Set aside.

In a large bowl with an electric mixer (or by hand, with a whisk), beat together the sugar, oil, eggs and vanilla.

In another bowl, stir together the flour, baking powder and cinnamon. Add this mixture to the egg mixture along with the shredded zucchini, stirring until the batter is evenly combined. It will seem too stiff and dry at first, but keep stirring and the zucchini will add enough liquid to loosen up the whole business. Spread batter in the prepared baking pan and sprinkle the chocolate chips evenly over the top. Bake for 25 to 30 minutes, until a toothpick poked into the middle of the cake comes out clean. Let cool completely before cutting into squares.

Makes one 8-inch (20 cm) square cake (about 16 servings).

Variation

Double Chocolate Zucchini Cake

Stir ¼ cup (50 mL) unsweetened cocoa powder into the flour mixture. Otherwise, bake as above. Bet you never thought zucchini was capable of such extravagance.

Easy Lemon Gingerbread Cake

It's a dark and stormy night. You need something warm and spicy to make you feel safe from monsters. This will do it.

½ cup	125 mL	milk
1 tbsp	15 mL	lemon juice
1 ½ cups	375 mL	all-purpose flour
½ tsp	2 mL	baking soda
2 tsp	10 mL	ground ginger
1 tsp	5 mL	cinnamon
1 tbsp	15 mL	finely grated lemon zest
½ cup	125 mL	light brown sugar
2		eggs
½ cup	125 mL	molasses
½ cup	125 mL	vegetable oil
		icing sugar for dusting

Preheat the oven to 350° F (180° C). Grease an 8 or 9-inch (20 or 23 cm) square baking pan. Set aside.

Stir together the milk and the lemon juice and let sit while you gather the rest of the ingredients. The milk will curdle and look quite disgusting. This is a good thing. Really, it is.

In a bowl, stir together the flour, baking soda, ginger and cinnamon. Set aside.

Now, dump the curdled milk, the grated lemon zest, brown sugar, eggs, molasses and oil into the container of a blender. Blend on medium speed until smooth, scraping down the sides with a rubber scraper once or twice. Add the flour mixture, then blend again, stopping the blender several times to scrape down the sides so that everything mixes together into a smooth batter. Pour into the prepared baking pan and bake for 30 to 35 minutes until a toothpick poked into the middle of the cake comes out clean.

Let cool slightly before dusting with icing sugar and cutting into squares to serve warm with whipped cream. Or cool completely and frost with Cream Cheese Frosting (see page 165).

Makes one 8 or 9-inch (20 or 23 cm) square cake (about 12 to 16 servings).

Ack! Disaster!

Your cake fell out of the pan, upside down onto the kitchen floor. Or the dog got it. Or it burned. Can it be rescued? Maybe. Maybe not.

Broken Cake

Half of your cake stayed in the pan but the other half didn't. Don't panic. It's nothing a little icing won't fix. Reassemble the pieces of cake on the serving plate and cover the whole business with an extra-thick layer of frosting, taking care to hide the seams and any bumpy parts. There. No one need ever know the truth.

Even More Broken Cake

Make trifle. Any kind of cake can be used as a base for trifle. Even chocolate. Everyone will love it, and no one will ever suspect it's not what you had planned. See trifle recipe on page 134.

Completely Disintegrated Cake

We don't want to know how it happened. Just put whatever's left of the cake into a food processor and whirl it around until it's chopped into coarse crumbs. Dump them out onto a baking sheet and place in the oven at 300° F (150° C) for 10 to 20 minutes to toast. Store in a plastic container and sprinkle on ice cream or yogurt.

Dog Got It

Yeah, it happens. Just cut off the chewed parts and cut the remaining cake into a creative, unusual shape. Cover with frosting, and don't say a thing to anyone.

Eek. It Burned!

As soon as you discover that your cake has burned, remove it from the pan and trim away all the burned parts with a sharp knife. Given time, the burnt taste will infiltrate the rest of the cake, so it's important to work quickly. If the rest of the cake still tastes OK, just cover it with icing and pretend it never happened.

It Fell into the Toilet. It Was an Accident—Honest.

Are you kidding? Forget it. Have ice cream. And be more careful next time.

Fruit-Swirl Coffeecake

Variation

Deluxe Crumb Coffeecake

Sprinkle the top of the cake with All-Purpose Crumble Topping (see page 176) before baking. Positively deluxe.

Better than anything you can get at a bakery. This coffeecake is especially delicious served warm.

8 oz	250 g	cream cheese, softened
1 cup	250 mL	granulated sugar
½ cup	125 mL	butter
2		eggs
1 tsp	5 mL	vanilla
1 ¾ cups	425 mL	all-purpose flour
1 tsp	5 mL	baking powder
½ tsp	2 mL	baking soda
¼ cup	50 mL	milk
½ cup	125 mL	any kind of jam (strawberry, raspberry, apricot, whatever)
		icing sugar for dusting or Shiny Sugar Glaze (see page 167)

Preheat the oven to 350° F (180° C). Grease a 9 x 13-inch (23 x 33 cm) baking pan. Set aside.

In a large bowl with an electric mixer, beat together the cream cheese, sugar and butter until smooth. Add the eggs and vanilla and beat until light and fluffy.

In another bowl, stir together the flour, baking powder and baking soda. Add the flour mixture to the cream cheese mixture in 2 or 3 additions, alternating with the milk, and mixing well after each addition. Spread batter in the prepared baking pan. Drop dollops of jam all over the top of the batter, then swirl the jam through the batter by gently running a knife through several times. Don't overswirl—you're aiming for a marbled effect, not a mucky mixture. Bake for 30 to 35 minutes, or until a toothpick poked into the middle comes out clean.

Remove from oven, let cool completely, then drizzle with Shiny Sugar Glaze or just dust with icing sugar from a sieve before serving.

Makes about 12 servings.

O␣ ␣ ␣ ␣ Buttermilk
Cof␣ ␣ ␣

*Yikes! It's y␣ ␣ ␣ ␣ ␣ ␣ row this coffeecake together the
night before ␣ ␣ ␣ ␣ ␣ ␣ nto the oven while you're taking your shou␣ ␣ ␣ ␣ ␣ ␣ e your guests arrive. One less
thing to think␣ ␣ ␣*

Topping

¼ cup	50 mL	light brown sugar
¼ cup	50 mL	chopped walnuts
¼ tsp	1 mL	cinnamon

Batter

1 cup	250 mL	all-purpose flour
½ tsp	2 mL	cinnamon
½ tsp	2 mL	baking powder
¼ tsp	1 mL	baking soda
⅓ cup	75 mL	butter
½ cup	50 mL	granulated sugar
¼ cup	50 mL	light brown sugar
1		egg
½ cup	125 mL	buttermilk or sour milk (see page 17)

Grease an 8-inch (20 cm) square baking pan. Set aside.

Mix together the topping ingredients in a small bowl—¼ cup of
the light brown sugar, the chopped walnuts and ¼ tsp (1 mL) of the
cinnamon. Set it aside.

In another bowl, combine the flour, the remaining ½ tsp (2 mL)
cinnamon, the baking powder and the baking soda.

In a third bowl with an electric mixer (or in a food processor), beat
together the butter, granulated sugar and the remaining ¼ cup (50
mL) of brown sugar until fluffy. Add the egg and continue beating
until smooth. Now add the flour mixture to the butter mixture (in 2
or 3 additions) alternately with the buttermilk, beating after each
addition. Spread the batter in the prepared baking pan. Sprinkle the
surface evenly with the topping mixture. Cover the pan with plastic

wrap and refrigerate for several hours or overnight. (Or you can bake it right away, if you prefer.)

In the morning, preheat the oven to 350° F (180° C).

Remove the plastic wrap from the pan and bake the coffeecake for 40 to 45 minutes or until a toothpick poked into the middle of the cake comes out clean.

Makes one 8-inch (20 cm) square cake (12 to 16 servings).

There, now aren't you glad you made that last night?

The Clueless Baker

Apple Cake

Wouldn't a nice moist piece of apple cake go well with that cup of coffee? Peeling the apples is the hardest part of making this quick cake.

2 cups	500 mL	all-purpose flour
3 tsp	15 mL	baking powder
½ cup	125 mL	granulated sugar, divided
¼ cup	50 mL	vegetable oil
1		egg
1 cup	250 mL	milk
3		large apples, peeled and cored
1 tsp	5 mL	cinnamon
1 tbsp	15 mL	butter

Preheat the oven to 425° F (220° C). Grease a 9-inch (23 cm) square baking pan. Set aside.

In a large bowl, stir together the flour, baking powder and ¼ cup (50 mL) of the sugar (please pay attention—this is only *half* of the total amount of sugar).

In a smaller bowl, whisk together the vegetable oil, egg and milk. Add the milk mixture to the flour mixture all at once, and stir just until combined. The batter will be slightly lumpy—this is fine. Pour the batter into the prepared baking pan and spread it out into an even layer.

Meanwhile, slice the peeled apples evenly into very thin wedges. Arrange these slices in overlapping rows (or zigzags or *whatever*), completely covering the top of the cake. Meanwhile, mix the remaining ¼ cup (50 mL) of sugar (remember?) with the cinnamon. Sprinkle this over the apples, then dot the top, here and there, with the butter.

Bake for 25 to 30 minutes, until the apples are soft when poked with a fork, and the top is browned. Cut into squares and serve warm or at room temperature.

Makes one 9-inch (23 cm) square cake (12 to 16 servings).

Orange Cappuccino Pudding Cake

This unpretentious dessert is, in fact, a highly complicated scientific wonder. Cake on top, sauce on the bottom—and it happens all in the privacy of your very own oven.

1 cup	250 mL	all-purpose flour
1 cup	250 mL	light brown sugar
2 tsp	10 mL	baking powder
2 tsp	10 mL	grated orange zest
½ cup	125 mL	orange juice
1		egg
2 tbsp	30 mL	vegetable oil
2 tsp	10 mL	vanilla
¼ cup	50 mL	semisweet chocolate chips
⅓ cup	75 mL	granulated sugar
¼ cup	50 mL	unsweetened cocoa powder
¼ cup	50 mL	instant coffee powder
1 ¼ cups	300 mL	hot water

Preheat the oven to 350° F (180° C). Grease an 8-inch (20 cm) square baking pan. Set aside.

In a bowl, stir together the flour, brown sugar, baking powder and grated orange zest. Add the orange juice, egg, vegetable oil and vanilla. Mix well until the batter is smooth. Pour into the prepared baking pan. Sprinkle the chocolate chips over the top.

In a small bowl, mix together the sugar, cocoa powder and instant coffee. Stir in the hot water and mix until everything is dissolved. Pour this brown liquid over the top of the *unbaked* batter in the pan. Yes, really. This will work. Bake for 30 to 35 minutes, until the cake feels springy when you touch it.

Let cool for a few minutes, then serve this disgustingly delicious dessert by scooping out some of the cakey part along with some of the saucy stuff. Vanilla ice cream is mandatory.

Makes about 9 servings.

Cake-Building ideas:

Start with a basic cake (or two), add some frosting, a glaze, maybe some fruit or whipped cream. What have you got? Well, lots of different things. Here are just a few ideas for building your own original cake creations.

Sacher Torte

Bottom layer: one half thickness chocolate layer

Spread with: apricot jam

Cover with: another half thickness chocolate layer

Top with: Chocolate Ganache Glaze (see page 166)

Black Forest Cake

Bottom layer: one chocolate layer

Spread with: canned cherry pie filling

Spread with: whipped cream

Cover with: another chocolate layer

Frost with: whipped cream

Decorate with: maraschino cherries and chocolate curls

Ice Cream Cake

(Layer cake and ice cream as follows in a deep springform pan, freeze until solid, then remove from pan and cover with whipped cream.)

Bottom layer: one half thickness chocolate or yellow layer

Fill with: two litres ice cream (any flavor, softened)

Cover with: another half thickness chocolate or yellow layer

Frost with: whipped cream

Classic Devil's Food Cake

Bottom layer: one chocolate layer

Fill with: sour cream (or regular) chocolate frosting

Cover with: another chocolate layer

Frost with: Sour cream (or regular) chocolate frosting

Multistriped Cake

Bottom layer: one half thickness yellow layer

Spread with: vanilla frosting

Cover with: one half thickness chocolate layer

Spread with: chocolate frosting

Cover with: another half thickness yellow layer

Spread with: vanilla frosting

Cover with: half thickness chocolate layer

Frost with: chocolate frosting

Strawberry (or Peach or Blueberry or Raspberry) Shortcake

Bottom layer: one yellow layer

Fill with: sweetened sliced berries or peaches

Spread with: whipped cream

Cover with: another yellow layer

Frost with: whipped cream

Decorate with: whole berries (or whatever)

Buche de Noel (Christmas Log Cake, if you really must know)

Lay two spongy roll cakes, side by side, on a large, clean dish towel; spread with filling and roll them (starting with the long side) to make one double-thick cake roll.

Begin with: two spongy roll cakes

Spread with: chocolate buttercream or whipped cream

Frost with: chocolate buttercream

Decorate creatively to look like a log

Frostings
Creamy Chocolate Frosting

This quick and easy chocolate frosting can be whipped up in no time and slathered on any cake you happen to have available. If there's any frosting left over, you can freeze it to use some other time.

1 cup	250 mL	unsalted butter or margarine, softened
½ cup	125 mL	unsweetened cocoa powder
½ tsp	2 mL	vanilla
2 cups	500 mL	icing sugar
1 tbsp	15 mL	milk (only if necessary)

In a large mixing bowl, beat the butter with an electric mixer until creamy. Add all the rest of the ingredients (except the milk), and beat on high speed until smooth and fluffy. (Add the milk, one molecule at a time, only if the frosting is too stiff. Remember—you can always add more milk if you need it, but you can't take it away if you've added too much.)

Makes enough to fill and frost a two-layer, 8 or 9-inch (20 or 23 cm) round cake. Or more than enough to thickly frost the top of a rectangular 9 x 13-inch (23 x 33 cm) cake.

Creamy Vanilla Frosting

Got a cupcake craving? Here's the perfect icing to put on top. And don't forget to lick the beaters.

1 cup	250 mL	unsalted butter or margarine, softened
1 tsp	5 mL	vanilla
3 cups	750 mL	icing sugar
1 tbsp	15 mL	milk (optional)

In a large mixing bowl, beat the butter with an electric mixer until creamy. Add all the rest of the ingredients (except the milk) and beat at high speed until smooth and fluffy. (Add the milk, one single molecule at a time, only if you feel the frosting is too thick. You can always add more later, but you can never undo the damage if you add too much.)

Makes enough to fill and frost a two-layer, 8 or 9-inch (20 or 23 cm) round cake. Or more than enough to thickly frost the top of a rectangular 9 x 13-inch (23 x 33 cm) cake.

Deluxe Buttercream Frosting

Variations

Chocolate Buttercream

Melt 4 squares (1 oz/ 28 g each) unsweetened chocolate and add to the butter mixture when you add the icing sugar. Increase whipping cream to ⅓ cup (75 mL).

Mocha Buttercream

Melt 2 squares (1 oz/ 28 g each) unsweetened chocolate and add to the butter mixture when you add the icing sugar. Dissolve 1 tbsp (15 mL) instant coffee powder in the whipping cream. Prepare recipe as for vanilla.

Coffee Buttercream

Dissolve 2 tbsp (30 mL) instant coffee powder in the whipping cream. Prepare recipe as for vanilla.

Although regular buttercream frosting will usually do the trick, this one is a notch above. It doesn't take much more time to make and turns out exceptionally creamy and fluffy, and even more irresistible than the usual kind.

1 cup	250 mL	unsalted butter or margarine
4 cups	1 liter	icing sugar
1 tsp	5 mL	vanilla
¼ cup	50 mL	whipping cream

In a large mixing bowl, beat the butter or margarine with an electric mixer until creamy. Add the icing sugar and beat until well blended. Add the vanilla and whipping cream and continue to beat on high speed until frosting is fluffy and creamy—about 5 minutes. (You can add up to 2 tbsp/30 mL of additional whipping cream if you feel that the frosting is too stiff.)

Makes more than enough ultra-creamy frosting to generously fill and frost a two-layer, 8 or 9-inch (20 or 23 cm) round cake. Or more than enough to thickly frost the top of a rectangular 9 x 13-inch (23 x 33 cm) cake.

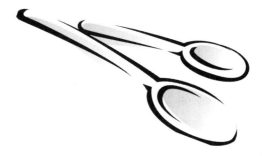

Fudgy Sour Cream Frosting

I know what you're thinking. You're thinking: ick. Sour cream? Fudgy? Well you'd be wrong. This is amazing. And possibly the easiest frosting you'll ever make. Try it on your next pan of brownies if you don't believe me.

2 cups	500 mL	semisweet chocolate chips
1 ½ cups	375 mL	sour cream
1 tsp	5 mL	vanilla

In a double boiler, or in a saucepan set over a pan of hot (not boiling) water, melt the chocolate chips, stirring until smooth. Transfer to a mixing bowl.

Add the sour cream and the vanilla and beat, with an electric mixer on medium speed, until smooth and creamy. Let cool just slightly— until the frosting begins to thicken. But don't wait too long because it will quickly thicken beyond spreadability, forcing you to resort to Plan B (see sidebar). Spread frosting evenly over cake or brownies, then chill until set.

Eat. Be happy.

Makes enough to fill and frost a two-layer, 9-inch (23 cm) round cake, the top of a 9 x 13-inch (23 x 33 cm) rectangular cake, or a couple of pans of brownies.

Plan B

The Fudgy Sour Cream Frosting is too thick. What now? Well, you can rescue it by heating it gently in a double boiler over simmering water, stirring just until it becomes spreadable again. Use immediately. And don't let it happen again.

Cream Cheese Frosting

A classic on carrot cake. Delicious elsewhere too.

½ cup	125 mL	unsalted butter or margarine, softened
1 cup	250 mL	softened cream cheese
4 cups	1 liter	icing sugar

In a medium bowl, beat together all the ingredients until fluffy and smooth.

Makes enough to fill and frost a two-layer, 8 or 9-inch (20 or 23 cm) round cake, or the top of a rectangular 9 x 13-inch (23 x 33 cm) cake.

Chocolate Ganache Glaze

This dark, rich chocolate glaze is strictly for the mature and serious chocolate lover. Glossy and smooth, not too sweet, dangerously delicious. It transforms an otherwise innocent cupcake into a public menace.

4 squares		(1 oz/28 g each) semisweet chocolate
¼ cup	50 mL	whipping cream
1 tbsp	15 mL	unsalted butter

If you have a microwave, combine the semisweet chocolate, broken into chunks, and the whipping cream in a small, microwave-safe bowl. Microwave on high power for 30 seconds, stir, then add the butter, microwave for another 20 seconds and stir until completely smooth. Let cool for 5 or 10 minutes before using.

If you don't have a microwave, combine the ingredients (as above) in a saucepan. Place over medium-low heat, and cook, stirring constantly, until the mixture is melted and smooth. Let cool 5 or 10 minutes before using.

Makes enough glaze for 12 cupcakes or one 8 or 9-inch (20 or 23 cm) round or square cake or a pan of brownies. The recipe can be doubled if desired.

To Glaze Cupcakes

Pour warm glaze into a small bowl. Hold each cupcake by the bottom and dip into the chocolate glaze, twirling it so the glaze coats the top of the cupcake. Place on a tray and refrigerate, without disturbing, until the glaze sets.

To Glaze a Cake or Brownies

Pour glaze evenly over the top of the cake, then spread while still warm, to cover the surface of the cake evenly. Refrigerate until set. (Don't mess with the glaze once it's set or else you'll ruin the effect.)

Royal Decorator Icing

This icing dries hard and white—ideal for decorating gingerbread or sugar cookies.

1 ½ cups	375 mL	icing sugar
1		egg white
½ tsp	2 mL	lemon juice

In a medium bowl, with an electric mixer, beat together all ingredients until light and fluffy. The more you beat, the better the icing, so don't worry about overdoing it. You can divide the icing into several bowls and tint them different colors if you insist on a multi-colored effect.

Keep the icing tightly covered with plastic wrap to prevent it from drying out until you're ready to use it. Makes about 1 cup (250 mL) of icing.

Shiny Sugar Glaze

The lemon juice version of this sugar glaze is especially good on fruit-filled coffee cakes or cookies.

1 cup	250 mL	icing sugar
2 tbsp	30 mL	water (or lemon juice)

In a small bowl, stir together the icing sugar with the water or lemon juice—adding the liquid a little bit at a time, until smooth. Spread on cookies or drizzle over coffeecake—then leave it alone until it dries.

That's it.

Makes almost 1 cup (250 mL).

Last-minute desperate cake decorating idea

Yikes! You made a cake but you don't have time to make icing. It looks so naked sitting there on the plate. Don't panic. Just spoon some icing sugar into a small strainer and dust your cake until the top is evenly coated. If you're feeling creative, you can place paper cutouts of stars or stripes or even a paper doily on top of the cake before dusting. Lift the stencil off carefully and voila! A *very* impressive design. Hardly looks desperate at all.

Clueless Troubleshooting: Cakes and Frostings

The last thing you need from a cake is trouble. But—alas—it happens. Despite the trauma of the collapsed birthday cake or the cracked cheesecake, you will live to bake again. Here are some ways to avoid a repeat performance of whatever disaster you just experienced.

It didn't rise at all.

- Did you forget to add the baking powder or baking soda? Are you sure?
- How old is your baking powder/soda? Is it the same package you bought when you moved into your house five years ago? Treat yourself to a fresh one—it doesn't last forever.
- Did you let the batter sit around for a while before baking it? Baking soda and baking powder begin working as soon as the batter is mixed. If not baked right away, the batter may get tired and simply give up. Get it into the oven quickly next time.
- Did you overbeat the egg whites (if the recipe calls for separated eggs) to the point of collapse? Next time, beat them only until they'll hold a peak when you lift the beater out of the meringue. Any longer and they fall apart.
- Were you a little, er, overenthusiastic when you folded the beaten egg whites into the rest of the batter? They have to be treated gently so as not to deflate them. It's better to leave a few white streaks in the batter than overmix the whole business.

It rose nicely, then collapsed.

- This can happen with some sponge or angel cakes, because they're so delicate and there's not much structure to hold the whole thing up. Next time, be sure your egg whites are stiffly beaten (but not overbeaten—see above), measure all the ingredients carefully and be sure to sift your flour.
- Did you take it out of the oven before it was fully baked? Do the toothpick test next time (see page 28).
- Don't open the oven door any more than is absolutely necessary.

Fluctuating oven temperature can annoy a baking cake, causing it to throw a snit and collapse.

Ack—it's all lopsided! The cake, I mean.

- Your oven may heat unevenly, causing some areas to be hotter than others. Rotate the pans in the oven midway through the baking time to help avoid lopsidedness. Turn them back to front, and switch oven racks. It may not totally cure the problem, but it could reduce it.
- Are your oven racks bent? Check them. If the batter is on a slant in the baking pan when you place it on the rack, it will turn out lopsided.
- Quick and dirty solution: If your cake will be covered with frosting, just slice off the lopsided bits to even it out. Who's going to know?

The bottom burned before the cake was done.

- If your oven heats unevenly, you can try moving your cake pans to a higher shelf next time. Or simply lower the heat by 10 to 25 degrees. Get an oven thermometer and use it. It can avoid a lot of aggravation.

The batter overflowed in the oven.

- Your pan was probably too small for the amount of batter. Check the volume of the baking pan, or measure the diameter to make sure you're using the correct pan for the recipe.

The dog ate my son's entire birthday cake! Now what?

- Is the bakery still open? Go there. Tell them I sent you.

The top (or bottom) of the cake is sticky.

- Cool your cake on a rack after removing it from the pan so that the air has a chance to circulate around it.
- Humid weather will cause a cake to absorb moisture and become sticky. Can't be helped.

My cheesecake cracked!

- You probably overbaked it. Reduce the baking time by several minutes next time you make it. The filling may not appear to be done, but it will continue to solidify as it cools. And it will have a creamier texture too.
- But hey—you can fix it. Sort of. Covering the top of your cheesecake with a thick fruit glaze (canned fruit pie filling—like blueberry or raspberry) will hide a multitude of evils. You can also spread the top of the cake with sweetened whipped cream, sour cream or a thick layer of chocolate glaze (see page 146).

Pies and Pastries

Pastry. The very word can strike terror in the hearts of otherwise brave and competent cooks. Nightmare memories of tough and inedible crusts, glutinous fluorescent fillings, creepy chemical flavors. Relax, it doesn't have to be that way.

Making a pie is not rocket science. In fact, it's easy as, well, pie. All you need is a reliable pastry recipe (or two), a few fabulous fillings and a little practice. It'll be fine, really it will.

Basic Pastry Recipes

Foolproof Plain Pastry

This recipe makes enough dough for five individual pastry crusts—tops or bottoms. Mix up the whole batch—it's no more work—and freeze the dough in individual crust portions, tightly wrapped in plastic wrap, for future baking.

4 cups	1 liter	all-purpose flour
1 tbsp	15 mL	granulated sugar
½ tsp	2 mL	salt
1 ¾ cups	400 mL	solid vegetable shortening, very cold (frozen, even)
½ cup	125 mL	water
1 tbsp	15 mL	vinegar
1		egg

In a very large bowl, stir together the flour, sugar and salt. Cut the vegetable shortening into chunks and add to the flour mixture in the bowl. Now with a pastry blender or two knives (see page 173), cut the shortening into the flour mixture until it is very crumbly and resembles coarse oatmeal.

In a smaller bowl, beat together the water, vinegar and egg until blended. Stir into the flour mixture, tossing gently until everything is evenly dampened and it forms a soft dough. Don't stir and don't mash—you want the whole mess to stay lightly mixed.

With well-floured hands, form the dough into five equal pieces, patting them into flattish disks and flouring the outsides well. Wrap individually in plastic wrap and refrigerate for an hour or two, or freeze to use some other time.

Makes enough pastry for five individual 9 or 10-inch (22 or 25 cm) pie crusts.

Cutting in Shortening

Sounds like something a tailor might do to your new pants, right? Wrong. This, in fact, is a method of combining the shortening (fat) into the flour when you make pastry or biscuit dough, in such a way as to leave little fat nuggets dispersed throughout the dough rather than blended in.

Why do we do this? Well, if you've ever poked a fork into a nice flaky pie crust, you'll notice that it crumbles into layers rather than breaking evenly like a cookie. Each eensy piece of shortening creates a tiny layer in the pastry dough—which is exactly what you want it to do. Tricky? Not at all.

So here's what you do: Dump your flour into a bowl, and combine it with any other dry ingredients (sugar, salt, spices, etc.). Cut the solid shortening (butter, margarine, lard, solid vegetable shortening) into chunks and add it to the flour. Now using an official pastry blender (a special utensil with wires or blades especially designed for this very task), chop the shortening into the flour, making smaller and smaller pieces until it's basically just a crumbly mess. (You can also use a couple of knives to do the chopping if you don't have a pastry blender—it's just a bit more awkward.) When it's all crumbly, but before it turns mushy, stop chopping.

Now, all that's left to do is add the liquid, and you're ready to roll out the dough. See, that wasn't so hard, was it?

Rich Cream Cheese Pastry

This pastry can be used for pie crusts and tart shells or to make delicious rugelach (see page 108).

2 cups	500 mL	all-purpose flour
1 cup	250 mL	unsalted butter
8 oz	250 g	cream cheese
2 tbsp	30 mL	granulated sugar

In a large mixing bowl, combine the flour, the butter, the cream cheese and the sugar. Cream together just until it forms a dough that can be handled, then divide into three equal pieces. With well-floured hands, pat the pieces of dough into flattish disks and wrap in plastic wrap. Refrigerate for an hour before using, or freeze to use another time.

Makes enough pastry for three 9 or 10-inch (23 or 25 cm) pie crusts, or 32 rugelach.

Flaky Sour Cream Pastry

This flaky pastry is perfect for making strudel (see page 197) or butter tarts (see page 190). It rolls out beautifully and is very easy to work with.

1 ½ cups	375 mL	all-purpose flour
1 cup	250 mL	unsalted butter, very cold
½ cup	125 mL	sour cream

In a large mixing bowl, combine the flour and the butter, cut into chunks. With a pastry blender or two knives (see page 173), cut the butter into the flour until the mixture is very crumbly and resembles coarse oatmeal. Add the sour cream, stirring the mixture just until it forms a soft dough.

With well-floured hands, divide the dough into two equal pieces, patting them into flattish disks and coating the outsides so they aren't sticky. Wrap in plastic wrap and refrigerate for an hour or two before using, or freeze to use another time.

Makes enough pastry for two 9 or 10-inch (23 or 25 cm) pie crusts.

Basic Graham Cracker Crust

This basic recipe can be used to make either a crumb crust for cheese-cake or a crumb crust pie shell. Easy as, um, you know.

1 ½ cups	375 mL	graham cracker crumbs (about 18 crackers)
3 tbsp	45 mL	granulated or light brown sugar
¼ cup	50 mL	butter, melted

Preheat the oven to 375° F (190° C).

Mix together all the ingredients in a bowl until everything is evenly combined.

To make a pie shell, squish the mixture evenly into the bottom and up the sides of a 9-inch (22 cm) pie plate, pressing the crumbs firmly so that they stick. (Super easy trick to do this: spread the crumb mixture into a pie plate, and smush down with a second pie plate to evenly distribute the crumbs in a neat layer.)

For a cheesecake crust, dump the crumbs into the bottom of a springform pan and pat it down into an even layer. It's not necessary to have the crumbs climb up the sides of the pan.

Bake for 8 minutes and let cool before filling.

Makes one 9-inch (23 cm) pie shell, or bottom crust for a large cheesecake.

Variation

Chocolate Wafer or Vanilla Wafer Crust

Substitute the same amount of chocolate wafer or vanilla wafer crumbs for the graham cracker crumbs. (This works out to about 30 chocolate wafers or 36 vanilla wafers, crushed.)

All-Purpose Crumble Topping

Make a batch of this crumble mixture and keep it in a container in the freezer. It can top an apple pie or crisp or be sprinkled over unbaked muffins or quick breads.

1 cup	250 mL	all-purpose flour
½ cup	125 mL	butter
½ cup	125 mL	light brown sugar
½ tsp	2 mL	cinnamon

Combine all the ingredients in a large bowl (or in a food processor), cutting the butter into the mixture until it forms a slightly sticky, crumbly mixture. Sprinkle over pie fillings instead of a top crust, use on top of fruit crisps or even sprinkle on top of muffins before baking. A million uses.

Bake according to whatever recipe you're using.

Makes enough to top one 9 or 10-inch (23 or 25 cm) pie or one batch of fruit crisp. (The recipe can be doubled so you always have some ready to use.)

Any-Fruit Crumble

Pick a fruit, any fruit (fresh or frozen)—apples, peaches, rhubarb, strawberries, blueberries, raspberries, plums (etc., etc., etc.)—mix up some crumble topping and bingo—almost instant dessert!

6 cups	1.5 liters	prepared fruit (see sidebar)
½ cup	125 mL	granulated sugar
3 tbsp	45 mL	cornstarch
1 recipe		All-Purpose Crumble Topping (see page 176)

Preheat the oven to 375° F (190° C). Grease an 8 or 9-inch (20 or 23 cm) square baking pan.

In a large bowl, toss whatever fruit you're using with the sugar and cornstarch. You may want to adjust the amount of sugar to suit your taste and the sweetness of the fruit. Dump into the prepared baking pan.

Sprinkle the All-Purpose Crumble Topping evenly over the fruit in the baking dish. Bake for 35 to 45 minutes, until the fruit is bubbly and the topping is browned. Remove from oven and serve warm with ice cream or whipped cream.

Makes 6 to 8 servings.

That's the way the fruit crumbles

Apples, peaches, pears: peel, core and cut into slices or chunks.

Plums, cherries: remove pits and cut into chunks.

Berries: wash and remove stems (if they have any).

Rhubarb: wash and cut into ½-inch (1 cm) pieces.

Pies and Pastries

Classic Double-Crust Fruit Pie

Start with enough pastry dough for a 9-inch (23 cm) double-crust pie (two single pastry crusts). See the recipe for Foolproof Plain Pastry on page 172 or use store-bought pastry. Roll one half out for the bottom, fill with your favorite fruit mixture (pick one!) and roll the other half out to make a top crust.

Apple filling

5 cups	1.25 L	apples, peeled, cored and thinly sliced
¾ cup	175 mL	granulated sugar (or more or less, depending on the sweetness of the apples)
2 tbsp	30 mL	flour
1 tbsp	15 mL	lemon juice
½ tsp	2 mL	cinnamon

Blueberry filling

5 cups	1.25 L	fresh blueberries, rinsed and stemmed (or frozen—don't defrost)
¾ cup	175 mL	granulated sugar
2 tbsp	30 mL	flour
2 tbsp	30 mL	cornstarch
1 tbsp	15 mL	lemon juice

Peach filling

5 cups	1.25 L	fresh peaches, peeled and sliced (or frozen—don't defrost)
¾ cup	175 mL	granulated sugar
2 tbsp	30 mL	flour
2 tbsp	30 mL	cornstarch
1 tbsp	15 mL	lemon juice

Rhubarb (or Strawberry-Rhubarb) filling

5 cups	1.25 L	fresh rhubarb, chopped, or half rhubarb and half sliced strawberries (or frozen—don't defrost)
1 cup	250 mL	granulated sugar
2 tbsp	30 mL	flour
2 tbsp	30 mL	cornstarch

Preheat oven to 375°F (190°C).

On a well-floured surface, with a rolling pin, roll out half of the pastry (one crust's worth) into a 12-inch (30 cm) circle, as evenly as possible. Carefully transfer it to the pie pan, folding the pastry in half or quarters to make it easier to handle (see diagram on page 180). Center the pastry in the pan and gently press it into place. Trim off the excess pastry overhanging the edges of the pan. Don't panic if you make a hole in the crust—just patch it up with a little bit of dough.

In a large bowl, toss together all the ingredients for the fruit filling of your choice. Dump into prepared pie crust, smushing the fruit lightly to fill the shell, and mounding it up a little in the center.

For a traditional double crust pie, roll out the remaining pastry on a well-floured surface into a circle slightly larger than the diameter of the pie plate. Remember—you'll need some overhang to seal the edges (you can always trim off any excess). Carefully transfer the rolled-out pastry to cover the fruit. Make sure it's centered over the filling and gently tuck the top crust pastry under the edges of the bottom pastry crust, rotating the pie plate a little bit at a time as you go around. Relax—you're almost there.

Now this is the fun part. *Firmly* crimp the top and bottom crusts together to make a fluted (technical term) edge. Or just press around the rim with a fork. This not only makes the pie look fancy and professional, but it also seals the juicy filling inside so that it doesn't leak all over the bottom of your oven. Cut 3 or 4 slits into the top of the pie to act as steam vents.

Bake for 50 to 60 minutes, until the fruit is soft (poke a thin knife into one of the steam vents to check) and the crust is golden brown. Let cool slightly before serving with, of course, vanilla ice cream.

Makes one 9-inch (23 cm) pie.

Make mine crummy!

Instead of covering your fruit filling with a pastry crust, try a crumble topping instead. Make a batch of All-Purpose Crumble Topping (see page 176) and sprinkle over the unbaked fruit filling instead of a top crust. Bake as if it were a double crust pie (even though it was a whole lot easier). Great if you're not a big pie crust fan.

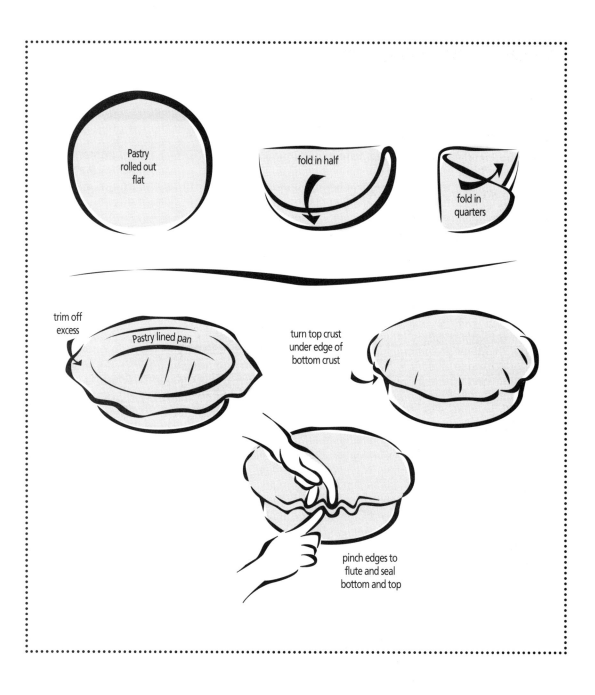

Pastry rolled out flat

fold in half

fold in quarters

trim off excess

Pastry lined pan

turn top crust under edge of bottom crust

pinch edges to flute and seal bottom and top

Killer Pecan Pie

Almost too much. But not quite.

1 cup	250 mL	corn syrup
⅔ cup	150 mL	granulated sugar
3		eggs
¼ cup	50 mL	melted butter
1 tsp	5 mL	vanilla
1 cup	250 mL	coarsely chopped pecans
1		unbaked 9-inch (23 cm) pie shell (home-made, see page 172, or store-bought)

Preheat the oven to 350° F (180° C).

In a mixing bowl, beat together the corn syrup, sugar, eggs, melted butter and vanilla with an electric mixer until slightly thickened—about 2 or 3 minutes. Stir in the chopped pecans, and pour the mixture into the prepared pie shell. Bake for 55 to 60 minutes, or until a knife poked into the center of the filling comes out clean.

Ridiculously easy for something so good, isn't it?

Makes one 9-inch (23 cm) pie.

Variation

Chocolate Pecan Pie

Melt 4 squares (1 oz/28 g each) semisweet chocolate with the butter in the recipe. Bake as above. Act nonchalant, if possible.

Impeccable Pumpkin Pie

Surprise bonus snack

This is guaranteed to be the best pumpkin pie you have ever tasted. No offense to your Mom.

Remove as much of the stringy pulpy goo from the pumpkin seeds as possible (close your eyes and pretend it's a human brain) and place them in a strainer. Rinse them under running water and dump them out onto a greased baking sheet. Sprinkle lightly with salt (if you want) and bake them at 300° F (150° C) for 30 to 45 minutes, stirring once in a while. Seeds should be golden brown and crisp.

Eat them on a stormy fall night, while watching a scary movie on TV.

2		eggs
1 ¾ cups	400 mL	pumpkin puree (canned or homemade—see page 183)
¾ cup	175 mL	honey
1 tsp	5 mL	cinnamon
½ tsp	2 mL	ginger
½ tsp	2 mL	nutmeg
1 cup	250 mL	canned evaporated milk
½ cup	125 mL	regular milk
1		unbaked 9 or 10-inch (23 or 25 cm) pastry shell (homemade, see page 172, or store-bought)

Preheat the oven to 425° F (220° C).

Place all the ingredients into the container of a blender and blend until smooth. Gosh, that was hard, wasn't it? Pour filling into the pie shell. (If you are using a 9-inch/23 cm pie shell, you may have a bit more filling than you need—use the extra to fill a few tart shells or bake in a custard cup as a bonus dessert.)

Bake the pie for 15 minutes at 425° F (220° C), then lower the temperature to 350° F (180° C) and continue baking for another 45 minutes, or until a knife slipped into the center of the pie comes out clean.

Cool to room temperature before serving with plenty of whipped cream.

Makes about 8 servings.

Start with an Actual Pumpkin? You've Got to Be Kidding.

No, not really. Here's what you do:

First of all you'll need a smallish pumpkin—about 6 to 8 inches (15 or 20 cm) in diameter—sometimes called a "pie pumpkin." Those great big Hallowe'en whoppers are too stringy and watery for baking. And besides, you left yours out on the porch to rot, didn't you?

Now, remove the stem and cut the pumpkin in half, top to bottom. Scoop out the seeds and place the pumpkin halves, cut side down, on a baking pan. Pour a little water into the pan—just enough to cover the bottom. Bake at 400° F (200° C) for 45 minutes, or until a little squishy to the touch. Turn the halves over and bake for another 10 to 15 minutes to dry them out a bit.

Remove from the oven, drain any liquid that may have collected in the pumpkin and let cool for a few minutes. Scoop the pulp out with a spoon, place in a blender or food processor and blend until smooth. That's all there is to it.

One 6 to 8-inch (15 or 20 cm) pumpkin should give you about 4 cups (1 liter) of pumpkin pulp, or enough for two pies and maybe a little extra (for pumpkin bread or something). If you're not going to use it within a day or two, freeze the pulp in recipe-sized amounts.

Chocolate Chip Cookie Pie

Imagine your favorite cookie. Now imagine it as a pie. This is it.

2		eggs
½ cup	125 mL	all-purpose flour
½ cup	125 mL	granulated sugar
½ cup	125 mL	light brown sugar
1 cup	250 mL	butter, melted and cooled slightly
1 cup	250 mL	chopped walnuts
1 cup	250 mL	semisweet chocolate chips
1		unbaked 9-inch (23 cm) pie crust (home-made, see page 172, or store-bought)

Preheat the oven to 325° F (160° C).

In a medium bowl, beat eggs until foamy. Add the flour, granulated and brown sugars, and mix with a whisk or electric mixer until blended. Stir in the melted butter and the walnuts. Pour into the prepared pie crust, and sprinkle the chocolate chips all over the top. The chocolate chips will sink into the filling—possibly all the way to the bottom. That's OK. Bake for 55 to 60 minutes, or until filling is puffed and golden but not dry.

Serve warm with ice cream or whipped cream. And, if you really can't leave well enough alone, perhaps just a drizzle of chocolate sauce.

Makes one 9-inch (23 cm) pie.

The Clueless Baker

Real Lemon Meringue Pie

This is the real thing. Made from actual lemons. You won't be sorry you made this.

Filling

1 cup	250 mL	granulated sugar
3 tbsp	45 mL	cornstarch
2 tbsp	30 mL	all-purpose flour
1 ½ cups	375 mL	water
½ cup	125 mL	freshly squeezed lemon juice
2 tsp	10 mL	grated lemon zest (or one lemon's worth)
2 tbsp	30 mL	butter
4		egg yolks, lightly beaten

Meringue topping

4		egg whites
¼ cup	50 mL	granulated sugar
1		baked 9-inch (23 cm) pie shell (home-made, see page 172, or store-bought)

Preheat the oven to 350° F (180° C).

In a medium-sized heavy saucepan, whisk together 1 cup (250 mL) of sugar, cornstarch, flour, water, lemon juice and lemon zest. Place pan over medium heat and cook, stirring, until the mixture comes to a boil and thickens slightly. Remove from heat and stir in the butter. Pour about ½ cup (125 mL) of this mixture into the bowl with the beaten egg yolks, whisk until smooth, then stir the whole business back into the saucepan with the remaining mixture. (This allows the egg yolks to gradually combine with the hot mixture and will prevent it from curdling—yuck.)

Return the saucepan to the stove and cook, whisking constantly, just until a few bubbles form in the lemon mixture. Remove from heat and pour into the baked pie shell.

Now prepare the meringue. In a mixing bowl, with an electric mixer, beat the egg whites on high speed until foamy. Gradually add the ¼ cup (50 mL) of sugar, a spoonful at a time, continuing to beat until the meringue forms stiff, glossy peaks. Spread over top of the pie, sealing the meringue to the edges of the crust to prevent it from shrinking as it bakes. Place in the preheated oven and bake for 10 to 12 minutes, until the meringue is golden brown. Cool, then chill before serving to allow the filling to set.

Makes one extraordinarily lemony 9-inch (23 cm) pie.

The Clueless Baker

How to Bake an Empty Pie Shell

You'd think it would be easy to bake an empty pie shell, wouldn't you? Just roll out the dough, lay it in a pie pan, slam it into the oven, and bingo! A pie shell!

Wrong.

A pastry shell does not like to be empty. Without a filling to make it behave, it gets all shrinky in the oven, slides down the sides of the pan where it sulks and bloats and becomes quite useless. The only way to get around this is to trick the pastry into thinking it has a filling. This is also known as "blind baking." Here's what you do:

Preheat the oven to 425° F (220° C).

Roll out the pastry and place it in a pie plate, as if you were planning to fill it. Cut a piece of foil wrap, waxed paper or parchment paper approximately the size of the pie pan and carefully lay it on top of the pastry to line the inside of the crust. *Act casual.* Now, fill the foil or paper-lined shell with about 4 cups (1 liter) of dry beans (chick peas are good) to weigh it down. Spread them out evenly over the pastry crust.

Put the bean-filled crust into the oven and bake for 10 minutes. This will partially set the crust. Now, take the pan out of the oven and remove the beans and the paper lining. Return the pastry to the oven and bake for another 5 minutes, or until crisp and light golden. Cool and fill. Ha. Outsmarted again.

Put the beans away, and you can use them over and over again anytime you want to blind bake a pie shell. Just make sure you label them so that you don't accidentally use them in your soup.

Pie-in-the-Face Cream Pie

If you are a circus clown, you will occasionally need to throw a cream pie. You can use this recipe, if you want—but frankly, for throwing purposes, I suggest store-bought.

2 cups	500 mL	milk
3		eggs
2/3 cup	150 mL	granulated sugar
3 tbsp	45 mL	cornstarch
2 tbsp	30 mL	all-purpose flour
2 tbsp	30 mL	butter
1 tsp	5 mL	vanilla
1 cup	250 mL	whipping cream
2 tbsp	30 mL	granulated sugar
1		9-inch (23 cm) graham cracker (or other crumb) crust (see page 175) (or a *baked* pastry shell) (see page 187)

In the container of a blender combine the milk, eggs, 2/3 cup (150 mL) sugar, cornstarch and flour. Blend until smooth, then pour into a medium-size heavy saucepan. Cook, stirring almost constantly with a whisk, over medium-low heat until the mixture becomes thick and smooth—5 to 8 minutes. *Do not* leave this stuff alone for a second! It will thicken suddenly and without warning—it's funny that way. Remove from heat and stir in the butter and vanilla, whisking until smooth. Cover the surface of the hot custard with a layer of plastic wrap (to prevent a yucky skin from forming), and refrigerate for an hour or two until completely cool.

With an electric mixer, beat the whipping cream with the 2 tbsp (30 mL) of sugar until stiff. Peel the plastic wrap off the custard and briefly beat it with the mixer so that it is smooth and creamy. Gently fold *half* of the whipped cream into the custard and pour into the prepared graham cracker crust. Smooth the top with a spatula, then carefully spread the remaining whipped cream over the custard.

Decorate the pie in a suitably attractive way—fruit, sprinkles, shaved chocolate, plastic spacemen, whatever.

Refrigerate for at least one hour before serving to allow the custard to set.

Makes one 9-inch (23 cm) pie.

Variations

Banana Cream Pie
Arrange a layer of banana slices (about 2 bananas worth) on the bottom of the pie crust before pouring in the vanilla custard. Decorate the top with more banana slices.

Chocolate Cream Pie
Add ½ cup (125 mL) semisweet chocolate chips to the milk mixture in the saucepan to make a chocolate custard. (If you are a hardcore chocolate freak, add 1 square (1 oz/28 g) unsweetened baking chocolate for a more serious flavor.) Decorate the top of the pie with chocolate curls (see page 139).

Coconut Cream Pie
Add 1 cup (250 mL) of unsweetened shredded coconut to the milk mixture in the blender. Decorate the top of the pie with lightly toasted coconut shreds.

Extreme Butter Tarts

Too much of a good thing?

Even if you only need a little bit of lemon juice for a recipe, you may as well go right ahead and squeeze the whole lemon. Freeze the extra juice in an ice cube tray and store the cubes in a plastic bag in the freezer to use another time. Same goes for grated lemon zest.

Just firm enough not to drip all over your shirt when you bite into one, but runny enough to be, well, utterly delectable. A timeless classic with no redeeming nutritional qualities whatsoever.

½ cup	125 mL	butter, melted
1 ½ cups	375 mL	light brown sugar
2		eggs
1 tbsp	15 mL	lemon juice
1 tsp	5 mL	vanilla
½ cup	125 mL	raisins or chopped nuts (optional—it's a personal thing)
24		unbaked tart shells made with either plain pastry (see page 172) or flaky sour cream pastry (see page 174)

Preheat the oven to 375° F (190° C).

In a mixing bowl, with an electric mixer, beat together the butter, brown sugar, eggs, lemon juice and vanilla until creamy and thick—about 2 or 3 minutes.

If you like raisins or nuts in your butter tarts—purists will object, but you can't please everyone—place about 1 tsp/5 mL into the bottom of each unbaked tart shell. Pour the filling mixture in, filling the shells almost (but not quite all the way) to the top. (If you prefer your butter tarts plain, just omit the raisin/nuts altogether.)

Bake for 18 to 20 minutes, until the filling is puffed and golden and the pastry is crisp and very lightly browned.

Makes two dozen tarts—enough to share. No really, you have to.

Hot Fudge Brownie Pie

This should take you about ten minutes to make. And no longer than that to devour.

3 squares		(1 oz/28 g each) unsweetened chocolate
½ cup	125 mL	butter
1 ¼ cups	300 mL	granulated sugar
¼ cup	50 mL	all-purpose flour
½ tsp	2 mL	vanilla
3		eggs

Preheat the oven to 350° F (180° C). Grease a 9-inch (23 cm) pie pan. Set aside.

In a medium saucepan, melt the chocolate with the butter over very low heat, stirring constantly until smooth. Remove from heat and add the sugar, flour and vanilla—beat with an electric mixer or whisk until blended. Now add the eggs, one at a time, beating until smooth.

Turn the batter into the prepared pie pan, and bake for 25 to 30 minutes, until just set in the middle, but not dry. The center should remain a little moist.

Serve warm with ice cream and, oh, go ahead, a drizzle of chocolate sauce.

Makes 6 to 8 servings. Or less.

Phyllo Pastry—It's Almost Cheating

Poor phyllo. Unfairly shunned for its finicky reputation, it is actually a remarkably easy pastry to use. So easy, in fact, that it's practically cheating. After all, you don't even have to make it yourself. So be brave—buy a package and make something. But don't be too smug. After all, there's really nothing to it.

Phyllo pastry is generally available as a frozen product. A 1 lb (454 g) package contains approximately 20 paper-thin sheets of pastry, rolled up and tightly wrapped in plastic to prevent it from drying out. To use it, you must defrost the package slowly, then handle the sheets of phyllo gently to keep them from tearing or becoming brittle.

Here's what you do: Remove the package of frozen phyllo pastry from the freezer at least 12 hours (or more) before you want to use it, and place it in the refrigerator to defrost. Don't try to defrost it at room temperature or in a microwave. Just don't. When you are ready to use it, open the box and remove the sleeve containing the pastry. Unwrap it carefully, then unroll the pastry leaves onto a sheet of waxed paper. Work quickly, using one sheet at a time, and keep the remaining pastry covered with another sheet of waxed paper and a dish towel to prevent it from drying out.

When you are finished making whatever you are making, re-roll the remaining pastry, slide it back into the plastic sleeve, seal it tightly and return it to the freezer (or keep it in the refrigerator for up to 2 weeks). Leftover unbaked phyllo pastry can be safely refrozen.

Phyllo Tart Shells

Fill these impossibly delicate tart shells with chocolate mousse, chocolate cream pie filling (see page 189), or even just whipped cream and fruit for a stunning, drop-dead dessert. Without actually dropping dead.

Preheat the oven to 350° F (180° C).

For each tart shell, you will need one sheet of phyllo pastry, thawed. (If you are making 6 shells, remove 6 sheets of phyllo pastry from the package, then re-roll the remaining phyllo and return it to the freezer. Yes, it's OK to do that.)

Stack the phyllo sheets on a cutting board and, with a sharp knife, cut out three 6-inch (15 cm) squares. Discard scraps. Cover the squares of phyllo with waxed paper to prevent them from drying out while you work with them.

Now, take one square (a single thickness of phyllo) and press it gently into the bottom of an ungreased muffin cup. The edges will overhang the top of the muffin cup. Place a second square on top of the first one, but position it in a slightly different way so that the points don't meet. And finally, place a third one on top of that, again arranging it so that the sheets don't quite overlap exactly. Press down lightly, and don't try to reposition the phyllo once it's been put in place.

Repeat with the remaining phyllo squares until you have used them all up—each tart shell having been made with a triple thickness of phyllo pastry. There.

Bake for 8 to 10 minutes, until the edges of the pastry are light brown and the shells are crisp. Carefully transfer to a rack to cool completely, then dust lightly with icing sugar or cocoa powder before filling them with something wonderful.

Try to be modest about it, please.

Baklava

The classic Greek pastry. Intensely sweet, very sticky, way too rich and much too buttery. In other words, absolutely perfect in every way.

4 cups	1 liter	finely chopped walnuts
½ cup	125 mL	granulated sugar
1 tsp	15 mL	cinnamon
1 lb	454 g	phyllo pastry leaves (1 package), thawed
1 cup	250 mL	unsalted butter, melted
1 ½ cups	375 mL	honey
1 tbsp	15 mL	lemon juice

Preheat the oven to 300° F (150° C).

In a large bowl, toss together the walnuts, sugar and cinnamon. Set aside.

Unroll the package of phyllo pastry onto a sheet of waxed paper. Cover with a second sheet of waxed paper and a clean dish towel. (The waxed paper will keep the phyllo from drying out and the towel will keep the whole thing weighted down and covered.)

Brush a 9 x 13-inch (23 x 33 cm) rectangular baking dish with some of the melted butter. Now, remove one full sheet of phyllo pastry from the stack and place in the baking dish, allowing it to extend up the sides of the dish. Brush with melted butter. Repeat until you have 6 layers of phyllo pastry in the baking dish, brushing each one with melted butter. Sprinkle with 1 cup (250 mL) of the walnut mixture.

Now, cut the remaining sheets of phyllo pastry crosswise in half. (A half sheet of phyllo should fit the baking dish almost exactly.) Place one of these half-sheets over the layer of walnuts in the baking dish. Brush with butter. Repeat until you have 6 layers of phyllo, each brushed with butter. Sprinkle with 1 cup (250 mL) of the walnut mixture.

OK, so far we've used half of the walnut mixture. Right? Repeat this procedure—6 sheets of phyllo, 1 cup (250 mL) walnuts, 6 more sheets of phyllo, another cup of walnuts, bla bla bla—until all the walnuts are gone. The top layer should be 6 sheets of phyllo pastry.

Trim away the excess phyllo pastry (the stuff that's sticking up from the bottom layer overhang) and brush the top with melted butter. With a very sharp knife, cut through the top few layers of pastry in a diamond pattern (4 long rows, then diagonally across) and bake for 1 ½ hours, or until the top is golden and crisp.

Meanwhile, in a medium saucepan, heat the honey with the lemon juice until hot but not boiling. Spoon the hot honey evenly over the baklava as soon as it comes out of the oven. Let cool completely before cutting into diamonds (along the pre-cut lines) and serving.

Makes at least 24 pieces.

Phyllo Pastry Apple Strudel

There is nothing like a slice homemade strudel. Unless it's another slice of homemade strudel. Go ahead—have seconds. No one is looking.

3 sheets		phyllo pastry
2 tbsp	30 mL	butter, melted
3 tbsp	45 mL	fine, dry bread crumbs
3		medium apples, peeled, cored and thinly sliced (2 cups/500 mL)
¼ cup	50 mL	granulated sugar
1 tbsp	15 mL	all-purpose flour
½ tsp	2 mL	cinnamon
2 tbsp	30 mL	chopped walnuts or almonds (optional)
2 tbsp	30 mL	raisins (optional)

Preheat the oven to 375° F (190° C).

Unroll the phyllo pastry and lay one sheet flat on a clean dish towel. Brush it lightly with some of the melted butter, and sprinkle it evenly with 1 tbsp (15 mL) of the bread crumbs. Place a second sheet of phyllo over the first, brush with butter, sprinkle with 1 tbsp (15 mL) crumbs. Cover with the last sheet of phyllo. Same deal—butter, crumbs.

In a large bowl, toss the sliced apples with the sugar, flour, cinnamon, nuts and raisins (if you're using them).

Arrange the filling in a 2-inch (5 cm) wide row, along one long side of the phyllo, about 1 inch (2.5 cm) in from the sides and long edge (see diagram page 198). Now, turn the bottom edge of the dough up over the filling to cover it, and fold in the two sides. Carefully roll the pastry away from you, using the dish towel to help you roll the strudel without tearing the phyllo. Transfer it as gently as possible to a lightly greased, parchment-lined baking sheet, laying the strudel seam-side-down. Brush lightly with the remaining melted butter.

Bake for 35 to 40 minutes, until the pastry is golden brown and the filling is tender. Let cool before attempting to remove from the pan.

Makes one strudel roll.

Flaky Sour Cream Pastry Strudel

You can also make a seriously delicious strudel using homemade Flaky Sour Cream Pastry (see page 174). The taste and texture will be different than a strudel made with phyllo pastry—slightly richer and not as flaky. To make one strudel roll, use half of one recipe of Flaky Sour Cream Pastry (freeze the other half for future strudeling, or double the filling and make two strudels).

You'll need:

½ recipe	Flaky Sour Cream Pastry (see page 174)
	Apple filling (as for phyllo strudel) or any other fruit variation (as follows)

Preheat the oven to 375° F (190° C).

Roll the pastry dough out on a lightly floured surface to a rectangle, approximately 9 x 15 inches (23 x 38 cm). It will be quite thin. That's fine—it's supposed to be thin. Sprinkle the entire surface evenly with bread crumbs.

Prepare the filling as for phyllo strudel, and arrange it in a 2-inch (5 cm) thick row, along one long side of the dough, about 1 inch (2.5 cm) in from the sides and long edge. (Clear as mud? See diagram page 198.) Now, turn the bottom edge of the dough up over the filling to cover it, and fold in the two sides. Carefully roll the strudel away from you, as firmly as you can without tearing it. Transfer it as gently as possible to a lightly greased, parchment-lined baking sheet, laying the strudel seam-side-down.

Bake for 35 to 40 minutes, until the pastry is golden brown and the filling is tender (poke a toothpick into the side of the strudel to check). Let cool before attempting to remove from the pan.

Makes one strudel roll.

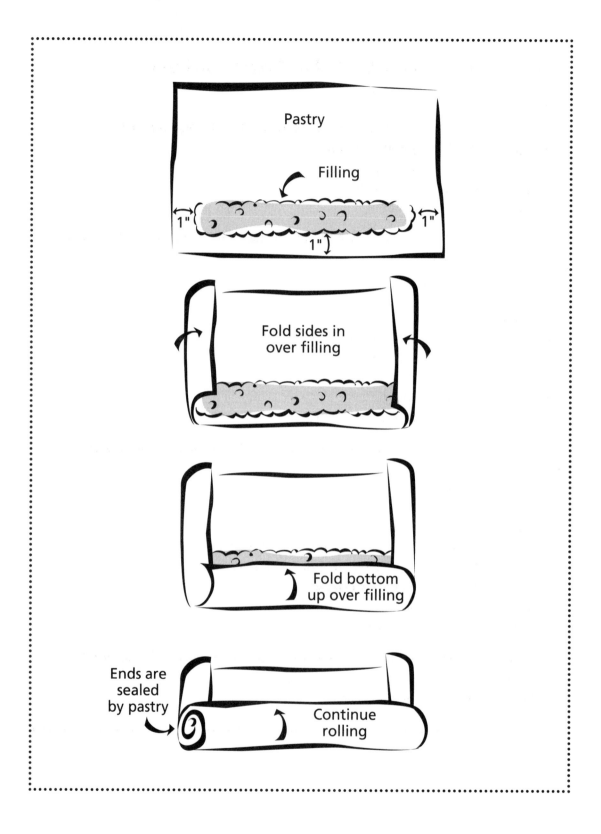

The Clueless Baker

So Many Strudels, So Little Time

Peach

3		medium peaches (about 2 cups/500 mL, prepared)
¼ cup	50 mL	granulated sugar
1 tbsp	15 mL	all-purpose flour
2 tsp	10 mL	cornstarch
¼ tsp	1 mL	cinnamon

Peel, pit and thinly slice the peaches. Mix with the sugar, flour, cornstarch and cinnamon. Toss to coat the peach slices evenly.

Makes enough filling for one strudel.

Blueberry

2 cups	500 mL	fresh (or frozen) blueberries
¼ cup	50 mL	granulated sugar
1 tbsp	15 mL	all-purpose flour
1 tbsp	15 mL	cornstarch
½ tsp	2 mL	grated lemon zest

Mix the blueberries with the sugar, flour, cornstarch and lemon zest. Toss to coat the berries evenly.

Makes enough filling for one strudel.

Strawberry Rhubarb

1 cup	250 mL	chopped fresh (or frozen) rhubarb
1 cup	250 mL	sliced fresh (or frozen) strawberries
⅓ cup	75 mL	granulated sugar
1 tbsp	15 mL	flour
1 tbsp	15 mL	cornstarch

Mix the rhubarb and strawberries with the sugar, flour and cornstarch. Toss to coat the fruit evenly.

Makes enough filling for one strudel.

Cream Puffs

Now what do I do? Cream puff ideas

• Fill with plain or Chocolate Whipped Cream (see page 150) and dust with icing sugar or drizzle with Chocolate Ganache Glaze (see page 166).

• Fill with ice cream and serve in a puddle of (store-bought or homemade) chocolate sauce.

• Fill with plain or chocolate pastry cream (see cream pie fillings on page 189) and drizzle with Chocolate Ganache Glaze (see page 166).

• Fill with sweetened sliced strawberries mixed with whipped cream (see page 150). Dust with icing sugar.

Astonish your friends and family with a batch of cream puffs. Let them think you are brilliant. Never let on how easy they are to make.

1 cup	250 mL	water
½ cup	125 mL	unsalted butter
2 tsp	10 mL	granulated sugar
1 cup	250 mL	all-purpose flour
4		eggs

Preheat the oven to 400° F (200° C). Grease two cookie sheets, or line them with parchment paper. Set aside.

In a medium saucepan, combine water, butter and sugar and bring to a boil over medium-high heat. Add the flour all at once, stirring constantly over low heat until the mixture leaves the side of the pan and forms a ball. Don't worry—you'll know what I mean when it happens. Remove pan from heat and let cool for a minute or two.

With an electric mixer, beat the eggs into the flour mixture one at a time, beating well after each egg, until the batter is smooth and glossy. The batter has a tendency to climb up the beaters—just scrape it down and keep going.

Drop the cream puff mixture by heaping spoonfuls (about ¼ cup/50 mL each) onto the prepared cookie sheets. Leave *plenty* of room between the blobs of dough for expansion. They'll puff to more than double as they bake. Bake for 35 minutes, then open the oven door and quickly cut a hole into the side of each puff to allow steam to escape, and continue to bake for another 5 minutes—until puffed, golden brown and crisp. Let cool completely, then, with a sharp knife, slice the top off about ⅓ of the way down. Lift off the lid, fill with something wonderful (see sidebar), then replace lid.

Makes 12 puffs.

Pavlova

This is an extraordinarily fabulous dessert. Much easier to make than you'd imagine, it can be filled with whatever fruits and berries happen to be in season.

Pavlova shell

3		egg whites, at room temperature
¼ tsp	1 mL	cream of tartar
¾ cup	175 mL	granulated sugar, divided (pay attention!)
2 tsp	10 mL	cornstarch
1 tsp	5 mL	white vinegar
½ tsp	2 mL	vanilla

Filling

1 cup	250 mL	whipping cream
2 tbsp	30 mL	granulated sugar
3 cups	750 mL	sliced fresh fruit (strawberries, raspberries, kiwi fruit, blueberries, peaches, bananas, mangos—it's all good)

Preheat the oven to 250° F (120° C). Line a cookie sheet or pizza pan with parchment paper (see page 81). Lightly grease the paper. Set aside.

In a large, scrupulously (even neurotically) clean bowl, beat the egg whites and the cream of tartar with an electric mixer until they start to form very soft peaks. (Turn the mixer off and lift the beaters out of the bowl—the meringue should be fluffy but still droopy.) Now, add half *(pay attention—only half!!!)* of the sugar, a spoonful at a time, while beating the mixture constantly until it forms a stiff and glossy meringue. (The mixture should be stiff enough to form a non-droopy point when you lift the beater out of the bowl.)

In a small bowl, stir together the remaining sugar (you do have some sugar left, don't you?) with the cornstarch. Very gently fold this mixture into the meringue using a rubber spatula, and being careful not to deflate the foam. Finally, fold in the vinegar and the vanilla.

Dump the meringue out onto the prepared parchment-lined pan

If at all possible, avoid making this dessert on a humid day—the meringue will absorb moisture from the air and become softened and sticky. Surely not what you had in mind.

and spread it evenly into a 7 or 8-inch (18 or 20 cm) circle. Build the edges up just a bit to form a rim. Bake for 50 minutes, then turn off the oven and let cool for 3 hours.

Prepare the filling. Beat the cream with the 2 tbsp (30 mL) of sugar until stiff. Spread in the cooled Pavlova shell and arrange the fruit on top. Serve as soon as possible after filling.

Makes 6 to 8 servings.

Clueless Troubleshooting: Pies and Pastries

Nice pie, kiddo. Too bad you had to feed it to the dog. Well, he liked it, anyway. Or maybe he didn't. Check behind the shrubbery. Well, don't give up hope—you learn from experience.

My pie crust is tough and chewy.

- You overworked the dough (you slavedriver!). Pastry dough should be handled as little as possible. You'll know for next time.
- Reduce the amount of flour slightly.

The pastry is really difficult to roll out without cracking.

- You may have added too much flour to the dough. Reduce the amount of flour next time you make it.
- Maybe it's too cold. Let it warm up to room temperature before rolling.
- You may be able to rescue the dough by kneading it a few times to make it more pliable and, if necessary, adding a few drops (just a tiny bit!) of water to moisten it.

The edges of the pie crust get brown before anything else is baked.

- This happens. If you want to avoid it, wrap the edges of the crust in a strip of foil halfway through the baking time. This will slow down the browning and keep everything an even color.

The fruit filling leaked out of the pie and all over the floor of the oven.

- You overfilled the crust. Reduce the amount of filling next time to avoid a blowout.
- If it was a double crust pie, maybe the edges weren't sealed tightly. Make sure you fold the top crust under the bottom crust, and pinch the two together firmly. You can also try moistening the edge of the bottom crust lightly with water before placing the top crust over it to form a better bond.

- But still, it's a mess. Just to be safe, next time place the unbaked pie on a cookie sheet or pizza pan before putting it into the oven. It won't prevent the leaking, but it will at least keep it contained.

My cream puffs collapsed

- The insides were probably still soft when you took them out of the oven. Next time, after they're finished baking, cut a slit in the side of each puff and leave them in the oven (with the oven off) for an hour to dry out.

The Clueless Baker

A Baking Glossary

Bake: To cook in an oven. But you knew that.

Batter: A goopy, semi-liquid mixture that when baked (see above) turns into something delicious: cake, muffins, cookies or whatever. You can't hold batter in your hand. Well, you can—but it will be a mess.

Beat: To mix ingredients energetically (like with an electric mixer), in order to incorporate air and make the mixture fluffy and smooth. Also to prove that you are the boss.

Biscuit: In England, this is a cookie. In the U.S., it's a small flaky quick bread. In Canada, well, it could be either.

Bread: Pretty much anything in a loaf shape. Some breads are sweet and cake-like, others are savory and, well, bready.

Brownie: Usually chocolate. Sometimes not. Usually a square. Occasionally not. Sometimes dense and chewy, sometimes light and cakey, always delicious. Even a bad brownie is better than no brownie at all.

Cake: Made with eggs and flour and sugar and butter. Multilayered and slathered with frosting. Flat and glazed with chocolate or dusted with icing sugar. A cake is, quite simply, magic. Ask any 5-year-old.

Chocolate: What? You need a definition? Oh, please.

Cookie: A tiny perfect cake. Rolled out and cut into shapes, or made from batter dropped onto a baking sheet. Any time of day is cookie time.

Cream: To beat together ingredients like butter and sugar (for example) so that they form a soft, creamy mixture.

Crimp: To make a pie crust look all frilly and pretty by pinching the edges with your fingers. Also known, in certain circles, as "fluting."

Crust: The part of a pie that little kids leave on their plates after scooping out the filling. Also the outsides of a loaf of bread that little kids don't eat. Is there a pattern here?

Cut: To mix solid shortening into flour by cutting it into teensy weensy pieces with a pastry blender or a couple of knives. An annoying but (alas) unavoidable technique in pastry-making.

Dash: Less than a pinch. But just.

Dough: A thick, pliable mixture of ingredients that can be rolled out and cut into cookies, or squashed into a pan to bake into bread. If you can hold it in your hand without making a mess, it's dough.

Dust: In cooking, to sprinkle lightly with a powdery ingredient, like icing sugar—a good thing. In housekeeping, it's that stuff that's all over the knickknacks in the living room—bad.

Flour: A powdery substance, made from grain. Most of our flour is made from wheat, but there are other flours made from rice, corn, buckwheat, oat, rye, soy (etc., etc., etc.). Flour forms the basis for most of our breads and pastries.

Fold: In baking, to blend one ingredient into another carefully and gently, by lifting in big strokes from underneath with a wide spatula. This technique is often used when adding something light and fluffy (like beaten egg whites) to a cake batter, in order to avoid deflating the mixture. In laundry, it's what you do with your T-shirts.

Frosting: The special part of any cake that makes it all worthwhile. Smooth and creamy, frosting can make the difference between just a nice cake and a total religious experience. It can also cover the part of the cake that the dog ate. But don't tell anyone.

Glaze: To cover with a thick, shiny coating—like chocolate or sugar glaze. Glazing a cake is a very effective way of covering up any number of horrible accidents. See also "frosting."

Grease: To coat a baking pan with a non-stick substance that will allow the cake you have slaved over to be removed easily. If it doesn't work, see also "glaze," above.

Knead: To pummel dough into submission, in order to force it to become smooth and elastic whether it likes it or not. Also recommended for stress relief.

Leavening: The ingredient in a recipe that makes the dough or batter puff up when it bakes. Yeast, baking powder, baking soda and even eggs can be used as leavening.

Meringue: This is the part of a lemon meringue pie that is required, by law, to be eaten first. It's made of a mixture of egg whites and sugar, beaten until stiff. Meringue can also be baked into crisp dessert shells and cookies, or formed into layers to use in tortes.

Mix: To stir together with a fork or spoon or, if all else fails, your hand.

Muffin: A small quick bread, usually sweet, that can be easily devoured in the car on the way to work or school.

Phyllo: A paper-thin pastry dough, usually bought ready-made (whew), that is used to make delicate pastries like strudel or baklava. Much easier to use than to describe.

Pie: A flattish, round pastry, filled with something or other. It may have a pastry crust, or a crumb crust. It might have apples in it, or chocolate cream, or chicken stew. There's no such thing as a bad pie.

Preheat: Go turn on the oven. Right now. Because you *are* thinking of baking something, aren't you? By the time your cookies are ready to go into the oven, it will be preheated to just the right temperature. Now wasn't that clever of you?

Shortening: Any solid or liquid fat. Butter, margarine, solid vegetable shortening, lard or oil are the types of shortening most often used in baking.

Sift: To pass flour or some other powdery ingredient through a fine screen to remove any lumps and fluff it up.

Stir: See mix. Same thing, basically. Except you usually do this with a spoon.

Tart: In North America, a tart is a tiny single-serving filled pastry shell. But sometimes a tart is a large, straight-sided European-style pie. And once in a while, it's that floozy with the short skirts who works down the hall at the insurance company.

Whip: To beat the living daylights out of egg whites or cream, making them foamy and thick. Like when you make meringue or whipped cream.

Whisk: A wire gadget for whisking. Or is it what you do with a whisk? Whatever. It's a lot like whipping.

Zest: The colored outer part of the peel of a citrus fruit—the yellow part of a lemon, the bright orange part of an orange, the green part of a lime. The zest contains a flavorful oil that packs a real citrus punch in baking. The underlying white part (called the pith) can be bitter, so don't use it when you're grating the peel.

Index